DEEP BLUE
Teaching
with Confidence

DEEP BLUE: TEACHING WITH CONFIDENCE

Copyright © 2018 Cokesbury.
All rights reserved.

No part of this work, accept as noted below, may be reproduced or transmitted in any form or by any means, electronic or mechanical, including photocopying and recording, or by any information storage or retrieval system, except as may be expressly permitted by the 1976 Copyright Act or in writing from the publisher. Requests for permission can be addressed to Permissions Office, 2222 Rosa L. Parks Blvd., Nashville, TN 37228-1306, faxed to 615-749-6128, or emailed to permissions@umpublishing.org.

Certain pages in this publication may be reproduced if the following permission line is included on them:
Permission to copyright for local church use only. © 2018 Cokesbury.

Scripture quotations are taken from the Common English Bible, copyright 2011. Used by permission. All rights reserved.

Writers: Laura Allison, Emily LaBranche Delikat, Daphna Flegal, Erin R. Floyd, Brittany Sky, and L. J. Zimmerman
Editor: Erin R. Floyd
Designer: Matt Allison

All Web addresses were correct and operational at the time of publication.

Print Version
ISBN: 9781501859588
PACP10527975-01
ePub Version
ISBN: 9781501859595
PACP10527976-01

18 19 20 21 22 23 24 25 26 27 — 10 9 8 7 6 5 4 3 2 1

MANUFACTURED IN THE UNITED STATES OF AMERICA

Contents

Preface—Teaching with Confidence

1. Deep Blue History, Philosophy, and Theology 1
2. Sacred Conversations 15
3. Using Deep Blue Resources 25
4. How to Set Up a Deep Blue Classroom 39
5. The Flow of a Deep Blue Session 49
6. Deep Blue Teacher Tips 61
7. Deep Blue Families at Home and at Church 77

Appendix—Using This Resource
to Train Deep Blue Volunteers

Deep Blue
Mission Statement

Reaching, empowering, and equipping children, and those who care for them, with grace-based resources that help them on the journey to

- understand themselves as children of God,
- explore and deepen their relationship with God through Jesus Christ, and
- love and serve God and neighbor.

B — BE WITH GOD
- Develop the sense that God is always with you
- Feel awe and wonder of God's mighty acts
- Know that God loves you and offers you grace

L — LOVE GOD AND NEIGHBOR
- Show love to family and friends
- Value the diversity among persons, recognizing the contributions that the variety of gifts, cultures, and physical abilities make to the community
- Participate in service projects appropriate to your age level and abilities

U — UNDERSTAND YOURSELF AS A CHILD OF GOD
- Develop self-esteem and know that you are worthy of love and care
- Join with others to worship God
- Develop a sense of belonging to the faith community

E — EXPLORE FAITH AND THE BIBLE
- Investigate, experience, and question your faith
- Find guidance for disciplines of prayer and Bible reading
- Grow in your understanding of the relationship between the Bible message and their own relationship with God
- Explore the meaning of commitment to God through Jesus Christ

Preface
Teaching
with Confidence

I received a tug on my heart and a call to ministry when I was a junior in high school. My youth group had traveled with the United Methodist Volunteers in Mission to Rio Bravo, Mexico, and instead of building a two-room house with the rest of our group, I played soccer with the children in the neighborhood and I held and sang to all of the babies. It filled me with energy, compassion, and love. I knew that God was calling me to serve alongside children for the rest of my life. This became incredibly clear in those moments playing with those sweet children. Looking at them was like seeing the face of God beckoning me to grace and love.

When I returned home to Oklahoma, I talked with my youth director, Matt Porter, about this call I had been feeling. He encouraged me to go to college and to take on leadership roles in our youth group. Before I knew it, I was attending Oklahoma City University studying Christian education in the Wimberly School of Religion. Through my coursework, mentorship from professors like Dr. Donald G. Emler, and an internship on the children's ministry team of a local United Methodist Church with Charlotte Teel, my call was confirmed. I was well on the path to becoming a children's minister, spending my whole life spreading the love of God to all of God's children.

This call has taken different forms during my professional ministry. From the local church to annual conference

Deep Blue: Teaching with Confidence

leadership to becoming a writer and editor at The United Methodist Publishing House, I have felt God's gentle tug. It is as if God was saying to me, "It's time to love my children in this new way, Britt." Each time this happens, I reflect on the moments in Rio Bravo playing with the children in the neighborhood. I remember the laughter and the feeling that God was all around us. Now, I try to discern how each next step or project will affect the children I have known throughout my life. I always want to be true to God and to the children God has given me the opportunity to know.

But the truth is I have always loved children. Their wonder, joy, and love is so honest. I always learn something when I spend time with kids. Whether it's a better way of looking at the world, a reminder of what's truly important, or a new insight to a Bible story, they teach me. It's a humbling experience to be a minister to children and their caregivers, because there is such a mutual give-and-take of wisdom, love, and grace.

Because of this mutual give and take, teaching children about our Christian faith can be an incredibly overwhelming task. It is something that requires care, preparation, and commitment. But I truly believe it is also one of the greatest experiences anyone can have.

I, along with the rest of the children's team at The United Methodist Publishing House, want you to be able to enjoy this beautiful opportunity to learn alongside your ministries. We want you to feel confident in the call God has given you to be in ministry with children. We always aim to give you all of the tools you need to do ministry well. From doing biblical research to testing games and crafts to integrating questions and rituals meant to create spaces of wonder in your class session to providing colorful visuals for additional implicit teaching, we have you covered. But we felt like we could do more to help—that's why we have put together this book and why we redesigned our sessions to be as easy to use as possible.

In this book, we will share our insights and tips, how our sessions and resources fit together, how to set up a classroom, and how to use this book to train additional teachers, volunteers, and ministry workers.

We will also share with you the theology and philosophy present in every resource we create. My hope is that this inside knowledge will give you a better understanding of what we aim to do through each session and story, and that you will get to know the creators of these products better.

To start, I have included a biography of each of the writers and editors on the children's resource development team. Each person also has included a story from her life about an experience she had with children. I hope we can share a piece of ourselves and work alongside you as we do ministry together.

We also want to get to know you better. *(This is a part of our theology and philosophy, which you will read more about in chapter 1.)* Please always feel free to reach out to us at any time. We are partners in ministry with you, and we want to be connected to what is happening in your congregation and community. You can email us through the contact page on our website (http://www.deepbluekids.com/about/contact.html), or talk with us and other children's ministers on our Facebook page (https://www.facebook.com/DeepBlueKids/).

My prayer is that God encircles you in love and grace so you can share that love and grace with every child God places in your care.

Sincerely,
Brittany Sky

Deep Blue: Teaching with Confidence

MEET THE EDITORS AND WRITERS OF DEEP BLUE

Laura Allison

Laura Allison received a BA in Biblical Education and Christian Education with a minor in Theology. She taught English and Math in a Christian school for eighteen years: first on the older-elementary level, then the middle-school level. Laura served four years on a local-church children's ministry staff and one year as children's ministry coordinator. She began teaching Sunday school at age fourteen and has served as a children's ministry volunteer for more than thirty-five years, specializing in Sunday school, Bible studies, children's church, children's choir, and vacation Bible school. She also has seven years experience at a publishing house as an editor. Laura is the writer and editor of Deep Blue One Room Sunday School and the editor of Deep Blue Large Group/Small Group.

During my years as a schoolteacher, one of my extra responsibilities was to write and produce school programs. Since it was a Christian school, our programs could be focused on Scripture. Most of the children loved playing parts in the programs, and I loved leading them. Over the years, God blessed me with many gifted and talented children to teach who blessed my life. One student who played leading parts in several programs was an accomplished singer. I watched him through his years in school progress and use his talent to serve God, and I prayed God would use him in a great way as an adult. Recently, I received a long letter from this student, along with two music CDs. I knew he had served as pastor in several churches, but he wanted to let me know that he is still singing. The two CDs were songs he had recorded, and they were amazing! And I shed tears of joy while I listened.

Teaching with Confidence

Selena Cunningham

Selena Cunningham holds an MA in English with a focus on writing from Belmont University in Nashville, Tennessee, and a BS in Communications from The University of Tennessee, Knoxville. She joined the staff at The United Methodist Publishing House as a production editor for Abingdon Vacation Bible School in 2011, and has also worked in Adult Teaching and Learning and Ministry Resources. She was previously marketing/public relations manager at Scarritt-Bennett Center, where she had an opportunity to be a part of promoting a variety of faith-based programs to the public. Her teaching experiences include work with grades 5–12 at a private Christian school, adult literacy tutoring, and serving as an adjunct professor at a state community college. Selena is the editor and writer of Deep Blue Older Elementary. She enjoys working with students of all ages and seeing them grow and excel. She dotes on her four young nieces and nephews, who are often "test subjects" for her educational activity and craft ideas (for work and sometimes just for fun)!

My favorite teaching experiences have been one-on-one encounters. It's great to get to work with a group, but nothing compares to working with an individual on a particular topic that he or she is struggling to comprehend and seeing the light of understanding and accomplishment spread across his or her face! I experienced this recently when I was given an unexpected and personal opportunity to teach. It was the day after Thanksgiving, and I had stopped by my sister's house with surprise donuts for her family.

Deep Blue: Teaching with Confidence

That afternoon, I found my eldest niece at the kitchen table working on her homework. Lucky for me, the subject was English! In particular, she was struggling with understanding the function of conjunctions in sentences and also how to identify prepositional phrases. While these may not seem like serious matters to adults (who know that, more than likely, no one is ever going to ask them to do these things again for testing purposes), to a child who knows that she will be tested, these can be very serious and stressful issues. I asked my niece some questions, reviewed her notes, and showed her an approach to breaking down the sentence structure that I suspect was a bit different from the one her teacher had taken. Neither approach was wrong, they were just different. The important thing is that learning was accomplished for the student.

The thing that I find most challenging and rewarding about teaching is pushing myself to find a way of explaining that meets the learner at his or her level—whether the challenge is breaking down parts of a sentence one-on-one or explaining a Bible story in a written lesson—so that understanding is accomplished and the student succeeds and moves on to greater achievement.

Emily Delikat
Emily Delikat holds an MA in Christian Ministries with an emphasis in Christian Education from Asbury Theological Seminary, Wilmore, Kentucky, and a BA in Music from Birmingham-Southern College, Birmingham, Alabama. Emily has more than ten years of experience in early childhood classrooms and worked as director of music, director of children's ministry, and director of spiritual formation in United Methodist churches before joining The United

Teaching with Confidence

Methodist Publishing House as a development editor. Emily is the editor and writer of Deep Blue Early Elementary and Deep Blue Kids Church. She is passionate about helping children and families fully participate in the life of the church through worship, education, and service. She lives in Franklin, Tennessee, with her family and attends Blakemore United Methodist Church. Emily loves to spend time with her husband, Andy, and her daughter, Maggie, and their guinea pig, Bucket. She enjoys reading, taking walks with her family, and watching way too much television.

For many years, I had the privilege of teaching preschool in church- and university-based children's centers. The days were long, exhausting, and fun. One of my students, Michael, was four and a big ball of energy. Sometimes Michael's energy was displayed positively and with curiosity. Sometimes his energy was displayed with frustration and defiance. One afternoon, Michael was angry because I had expressed that I felt it was important for him to use the bathroom instead of the playground garden when he needed a potty break. In the midst of a particularly difficult tantrum and cool-down for Michael, he decided to sit down on the ground next to where I was standing. He was quiet for a few moments, and then he looked up and smiled. He said, "Ms. Emily, you have a lovely shadow! I think I'm ready to go inside to the bathroom now." I had never before, and have never since, been complimented on the loveliness of my shadow. I don't know why Michael chose to compliment my shadow that day, but I think about him sometimes when I feel frustrated. Maybe all he needed was to sit in someone's shadow where he was safe to work through his frustration. His compliment reminds me of Psalm 36:7, "Your faithful love is priceless, God! Humanity finds refuge in the shadow of your wings."

_ _ _ _ Deep Blue: Teaching with Confidence _ _ _ _ _

Daphna Flegal
Daphna Flegal holds an MA in Christian Education with an emphasis in Children's Ministry from Scarritt College, Nashville, Tennessee, and a BA in Christian Education from Pfeiffer College, Misenheimer, North Carolina. She is a diaconal minister in The United Methodist Church. Daphna worked as director of children's ministry, director of Christian education, and director of programs in United Methodist churches for sixteen years before joining The United Methodist Publishing House as lead development editor. Daphna is the editor and writer of Deep Blue Preschool, and writes and edits our seasonal children's books. She has been a Sunday school teacher for two-year-olds, three-year-olds, and four-year-olds, as well as elementary children in her own local church, Connell Memorial United Methodist. Daphna admits she has a favorite student at the church—her granddaughter, Ginny!

I have served four churches as director of children's ministries and continued serving in two churches as a volunteer. The first church I served was First United Methodist in Midland, Michigan. I worked with a terrific professional staff and over a hundred volunteers.

During one vacation Bible school, we were learning about some of the people Jesus met. My volunteers and I created a Bible-times village. On the first day of VBS, the children made money bags out of vinyl and lacing, along with clay coins. Each child received several coins to put in her or his bag. When the children came to VBS on the second day they were greeted at the door by Zacchaeus, the tax collector. The children all had to give Zacchaeus some of their coins to pay their taxes. On the third day, Zacchaeus returned. The children were not happy to see him. Some children even hid their remaining coins in their socks! Fortunately, this was the day Zacchaeus met Jesus. After telling the children how Jesus had changed his life, Zacchaeus gave the children their coins back. The children were thrilled when Zacchaeus gave them twice as many coins as they had paid in taxes.

Erin Floyd

Erin Floyd holds a BA in Religious Education from Oklahoma City University and is pursuing an MA of Christian Education from Garrett-Evangelical Theological Seminary. Before coming to The United Methodist Publishing House, Erin worked for eight years in the local church, serving as the director of children's ministries and as the director of educational ministries at St. Stephen's UMC in Norman, Oklahoma. Erin is now the writer and editor of the Deep Blue Middle Elementary resources. She also serves as the children's coordinator at Blakemore UMC in Nashville. Erin is passionate about child and faith development, and is excited to be a part of an amazing team at The United Methodist Publishing House. In her free time, she enjoys journaling, taking walks, volunteering, and trying new coffee shops.

I had just picked up from school the two boys I nanny, and we were driving home. The older one, who is almost five, told me he had learned something new—his teacher had taught him something and asked if he could teach it to me. He wanted to teach me about how plants grow. I told him I would love to learn something new and that anyone could be a teacher. He shared with me his newly acquired information about seeds and plants, and I then suggested he teach his brother. I thanked him for teaching me, and he said, "Of course. That's the circle of life."

Sally Hoelscher

Sally Hoelscher lives in Iowa City, Iowa, where she is a freelance writer and Christian educator. Sally has written curriculum for all age levels and has been involved in ministry with children, youth, and adults for over thirty years, in both volunteer and paid positions. Sally currently writes the Deep Blue Large Group/Small Group curriculum and has written some of the Deep Blue Rotation Stations units. Sally holds a BS in Pharmacy from Drake University and a PhD in Pharmacology from the University of Iowa. Given her educational background, Sally is particularly fond of including science and math activities in her writing.

One of the things I enjoy about teaching is receiving insight from my students. Given opportunity and encouragement, young people are capable of sharing a great deal of wisdom. Recently while leading an activity that invited students to use their imagination to place themselves in a Bible story, one of the participants told me, "I like to use my imagination. No one can tell you that you are wrong when you are using your imagination."

Brittany Sky

Brittany Sky holds a Bachelor of Arts in Christian Education from Oklahoma City University and a Master of Arts in Christian Education from Garrett-Evangelical Theological Seminary. Before coming to The United Methodist Publishing House, Brittany worked as a minister with children and their families in local UM congregations and taught children's ministry workshops for the Oklahoma Annual Conference. She is now the senior editor of children's resources, tasked with leading the children's unit to create resources that are relevant and resonant for today's church and children. Brittany is also the writer and editor of Deep Blue Nursery. Brittany attends East End UMC and continues to explore approaches to Christian education that create vibrant experiences with God for kids.

When I served at St. Luke's UMC in Oklahoma City, part of my job was to lead the chapel services for our childcare center. It was one of my favorite things each week! The children would come to the church's chapel one class at a time. One Wednesday morning, one of the toddler classes came to chapel. I could hear them as they approached, but as soon as they were led through the chapel doors, the whole group grew quiet with awe. They walked to the front of the chapel and sat on the floor with me. We sang "Jesus Loves Me" together, passed a stuffed lamb toy around as we shared whether we were happy or sad that day, and then sang "God Loves Me So." At the end of the service, we shared a blessing with each other. I drew a cross on each extended hand, saying, "God loves you. God blesses you. God will always be with you." We said a prayer together and the children ran off to go back to class. But the reverence of this moment with toddlers is still with me. They worshipped God with open hearts, more so than many adults I know.

L. J. Zimmerman

L. J. Zimmerman holds a Bachelor of Arts in Religious Studies from the University of Pennsylvania, and a Master of Divinity from Candler School of Theology at Emory University. Before coming to The United Methodist Publishing House, L. J. served as a Christian educator and minister to children, youth, and adults in various congregations. She is the writer and editor of Submerge: Deep Blue for Tweens and editor of Deep Blue Rotation Stations. L. J. teaches and learns with children and

Deep Blue: Teaching with Confidence

youth in her local Quaker meeting. She loves biking around Nashville, knitting sweaters, and hiking with her dog, Memphis.

Once I took a group of fifth- and sixth-graders to make dinner at a homeless shelter. As the kids went about their various tasks, one kid lay down on the kitchen floor and muttered the word "spoon" over and over. I saw his mom watching his strange behavior with anxiety as she stirred a pot of soup. I knelt down beside him and said, "Isn't it weird when you say one word so much that it starts to sound like it's not even a word?" We started repeating various words, and soon all the tweens were practicing. The kid got up from the floor and joined his peers. Later, his mom thanked me through tears as she described how worried she was about her son fitting in. This is what I love so much about ministry with tweens: when everyone is willing to be a little odd, no one has to be the odd one out. Tweens are awkward weirdos with big hearts, ready to follow Jesus' call to radical inclusion. ○

① Deep Blue
History, Philosophy, and Theology

Brittany Sky

From the very beginning of the Wesleyan movement, John Wesley, and the American Methodists, felt it was important for all people to have access to books that helped followers of Jesus grow in their Christian faith. At the General Conference meeting in 1787, the delegates voted to establish the Methodist Book Concern, the first agency of the Methodist Church. In 1789, with six hundred dollars, John Dickins started producing pamphlets and books to help people on their Christian journey. What would later become The United Methodist Publishing House was established.

We have a 229-year tradition of "Reaching more people in more places with quality services and resources that help them come to know and deepen their knowledge of God through Jesus Christ, learn to love God, and choose to serve God and neighbor." Of those years, we have been creating resources for children and family ministries for 191 years.

The Book Concern had been publishing *The Christian Advocate* for six months when it began running advertisements for *The Child's Magazine*. The magazine began its circulation in 1827 and "intended to embrace in this little work short practical essays, anecdotes, narratives, accounts of the conversion and happy deaths of children, facts illustrative of the conduct of Providence, sketches of natural history, poetry, &c. The constant aim in conducting this little work, will be to lead the infant mind to the knowledge of God our Saviour."[1]

While we no longer publish the "happy deaths of children" (I mean, what on earth?), we continue to aim to help children come to know God.

The people who came before the current group of children's editors left a long legacy of creating curriculum and other written resources that promote grace-filled learning encounters with God. These folks, many of whom were female theologians and educators, were all very creative—integrating theology, educational theory, and spirituality into resources for churches to pick up and use in their children's Sunday school classrooms. (It is quite humbling to me to be a cog in this very big, long-lasting machine.)

To honor the work of all those who have come before, we have intentionally kept the underlying theology that has always gone into our materials and have fashioned a mission statement to articulate what we always aim to do through our ministry by

Reaching, empowering, and equipping children, and those who care for them, with grace-based resources that help them on the journey to
- **understand themselves as children of God,**
- **explore and deepen their relationship with God through Jesus Christ, and**
- **love and serve God and neighbor.**

---
[1] James Penn Pilkington, *The Methodist Publishing House: A History Volume I* (Nashville, TN: Abingdon Press, 1968), 209.

Deep Blue History, Philosophy, and Theology

Every book, session, and video that we publish is measured against this mission. If a proposed resource doesn't help us accomplish this goal, or seeks to undermine this goal, we don't create it.

We also have a guiding document called "Elements of a Core Curriculum for Children." (You can find the full document, along with other free teacher resources, online at http://www.deepbluekids.com/resources/2/free-stuff-for-teachers.) Our core curriculum document outlines

- our objectives for children, parents, and teachers,
- the general areas of content covered in our curricula,
- specific learnings and experiences we believe children need to grow in their faith,
- what each age-level and stage of development needs in order to create these experiences,
- a list of Bible stories every child should experience,
- a list of faith vocabulary that every child should know,
- a list of faith images and symbols important for children to learn, and
- a list of contemporary discipleship issues that children will experience.

These areas of content are covered through our vast and ever-growing library of resources and curricula. I would like to encourage you to review this document at some point, but I will also highlight some of the key points in it.

OBJECTIVES

Children will

- experience the awe and mystery of God's love, especially as experienced through Jesus Christ; identify themselves as children of God, the recipients of that love; and respond to that love by commitment to God through Jesus Christ within the community of faith.
- know the Bible and make its stories, people, passages, and verses a part of their lives.
- learn skills for using the Bible so that its message can be accessible to them.
- experience the faith community through the worshipping and serving life of the church, especially within their local congregations, and also connecting with persons of faith both past and present.
- grow in discipleship, exploring the calls of God, the teachings of Jesus, and the witness of the church as they participate in worship and other spiritual disciplines, decision-making, service, and witness.
- address with the riches of the faith the life issues that concern them and those who care about children.
- value the diversity among persons, recognizing the contributions that the variety of gifts, cultures, and physical abilities make to the community.

Parents and caregivers will

- find help for their own faith and life skills, empowering them to model and speak about their faith with their children.

Teachers will
- be nurtured in the Christian faith, enabling them to grow in faith and in their ability to model and speak about their faith, especially with children.
- be equipped with the skills and understandings needed to teach effectively.

Pastors and congregations will
- recognize children as an integral part of a vital community of faith and value their participation in worship, mission and service, and fellowship, as well as in the specific settings of children's ministries.

All adults will
- be advocates for children in the communities and world in which they live.

GENERAL AREAS OF CONTENT

The Bible—its stories, people, passages, and verses; the message of the Bible as a whole; the life, death, and resurrection of Jesus; and skills for using and understanding the Bible.

The Church—its beginnings; the heritage of our denomination; its practices of worship; its sacraments; its call to service, mission, and outreach; and the relationships found in the community of faith.

Christian Identity—commitment to God; commitment to Jesus Christ; commitment to the church; commitment to the practice of spiritual disciplines; a life of faith; and commitment to one's own ministry.

Christian Living—self-esteem based on knowing oneself to be a child of God; relationships with others and with the natural world; ethical decision-making; coping with difficulties; and the skills of critical thinking.

SPECIFIC LEARNINGS AND EXPERIENCES FOR GROWING IN THE FAITH

In order to create a more complete picture of what core curriculum is, we can identify some of the specific knowledge, skills, relationships and experiences, and attitudes and values that children need in order to experience God's grace, recognize themselves as children of God, and discover their calling as ministers of the Christian faith in their families, schools, churches, communities, and world. All of the Deep Blue–branded products have been created and published to help us accomplish this mission and to meet these objectives.

Knowledge
- Bible stories
- Bible passages and verses
- Faith heritage, which includes stories of the history and development of the Christian church, stories from the children's denominational heritage, and stories from the development of their own congregations
- Language of the faith, including not only special words, but symbols, images, and concepts
- The story of Jesus' life, death, and resurrection
- The elements of worship (sacraments, hymns, traditions, and so forth)

_ _ _ _ _Deep Blue History, Philosophy, and Theology _ _ _ _ _

Skills
- Coping skills
- Bible-use skills, such as being able to find books, chapters, and verses
- Decision-making
- Skills in using Bible-study tools, such as atlases, biblical maps, concordances, and dictionaries
- Prayer

Relationships and Experiences
- Relationships with loving, caring adults who help children experience trust
- Parents, teachers, and other adults who speak about their faith and model faithful living
- Positive relationships with their peers
- Baptism
- Caring support of a Christian congregation
- Experiences of being nurtured
- Participation in acts of service
- Opportunities to help others
- A sense of belonging
- Being forgiven and forgiving others
- Acceptance and participation in the community of faith
- Prayer
- Commitment (to God, to Jesus Christ, to the church, to one's own ministry)
- Awe and mystery of God's love
- Awe in the experience of God's creation

- Christian living in response to Christian learning
- Experiences of the reality of living in a multicultural world
- Opportunities to be creative
- Giving

Attitudes and Values
- Self-esteem
- Identity as a child of God
- Reverence for God's world
- A sense of responsibility for the natural world
- Valuing of the diversity among persons
- Respect for the rights of others
- An understanding that God expects us to act toward others in fair, kind, and loving ways
- Awareness that God is with us wherever we are
- Knowing that we are called to be followers of Jesus
- Recognition that the Bible is God's Word
- Belief that every person is important to God
- Concern for meeting human needs
- Christian attitudes and values reflected in responses to a variety of contemporary discipleship issues

DEEP B.L.U.E.

I was serving in the local church as the director of younger children's ministry when the Common English Bible (CEB) translation team (a brand and ministry team at The United Methodist Publishing House) put out the *CEB Deep Blue Kids Bible*. I had been looking for Bibles to give on Third-Grade

Deep Blue History, Philosophy, and Theology

Bible Sunday, but wasn't very pleased with the kids' Bibles on the market. They were all translated to a reading level that was far above a third-grade reading level. Several were condescending in the notes written in the margins to children from a lack of respect for children's curiosity and spirituality. Some had confusing imagery or really played to the "girls are all pink and boys are all blue" stereotypes. I just wasn't happy with anything I was finding.

That was until I got my hands on a copy of the *CEB Deep Blue Kids Bible*. The readability editor, Elizabeth Caldwell—a children's minister and professor—did a great job making the Bible common English for kids. The notes were respectful of the faith of children. The images showed a diverse group of kids exploring the Bible together, asking questions about Scripture, and wondering together about faith. It is an INCREDIBLE Bible.

When I moved to Nashville to be the GROW Early Elementary writer and editor, GROW had just begun. It was a fun curriculum that lived out the theology and philosophy of our team and church, but the team was already thinking about what would come after the three years of GROW were completed. I remember talking to some teammates about how cool it would be to have a curriculum that went with the *CEB Deep Blue Kids Bible*. We put together the proposal, and we got to work envisioning a Deep Blue–branded curriculum that provided opportunities for children to be with God, love God and neighbor, understand themselves as children of God, and explore faith and the Bible.

Be with God

All of the Deep Blue resources seek to create opportunities for children and their caregivers (teachers, parents, grandparents, foster parents, neighbors, and so forth) to come into contact with God. We intentionally choose stories, learning activities, and spiritual practices that create inbreakings for the Spirit to move. (Though we know the Spirit moves however the Spirit wants.)

Each quarter, all of the writers and editors gather together to prayerfully think through what each of the upcoming thirteen sessions will be. For each session, we begin by reading the Scripture in a Common English Bible and any of the accompanying notes the CEB team included about the passage. (There are so many great CEB products with fantastic notes!) We then review Bible commentaries, archaeological resources, and any new academic articles that have been put out. We each describe what theological themes we hear and think should be included in our session. Once we have these theological objectives, we talk through how these objectives could be experienced. Utilizing multiple-intelligence theory, we create activities that teach through visuals, music, movement, art, verbal reasoning, logic, interpersonal relationship-building, and intrapersonal soul-building.

We trust that through this spiritual practice of creatively creating curriculum, God will show up in our minds, hearts, and hands as we write. From these written words, caregivers will lead sessions for children to be with God.

Love God and Neighbor

In Luke 10:27, Jesus responded to the legal expert's question about gaining eternal life by saying, *"You must love the Lord your God with all your heart, with all your being, with all your strength, and with all your mind, and love your neighbor as yourself."* As followers of Jesus, we must teach our children through modeling loving God and neighbor. This means setting an example children can follow so they, too, can embody the spirit of service and care for all.

We believe that being a Christian (a Christ follower) means following the example of Jesus. Throughout the Gospels, Jesus learns, grows, and serves others. By teaching our stories of faith and giving children opportunities to serve, we help children learn to love God and neighbor.

Because this is so important to our faith development, we include missional opportunities every quarter. We also encourage each congregation to invite the children to serve (alongside trusted adults) at church and at local community organizations. By participating in service, we also have chances to be with God through loving relationships.

Understand Themselves As Children of God

We believe that every human is a child of God. Because of this, every human has inherent worth, deserves love and respect, and is valuable just for existing. Every session we write is written from this viewpoint. It aligns with what John Wesley called prevenient grace. "Wesley understood grace as God's active presence in our lives. This presence is not dependent on human actions or human response. It is a gift—a gift that is always available, but that can be refused" (http://www.umc.org/what-we-believe/our-wesleyan-heritage). Because of this grace freely given by God to all humans, regardless of what humanity does, we do not write activities that are in any way condemning or shaming. Instead, everything is written to empower and encourage children to recognize their infinite worth. Through this loving experience, children come to know they are a part of God's family.

Explore Faith and the Bible

Our faith is rooted in the stories of the Bible and the stories of our Christian foremothers and forefathers. These stories guide us on the Christian journey. They help us make choices that show God's love to all of creation. They inspire us to stand up for justice. They give us examples to draw on when life is hard. This vast library of stories grounds us in our faith. Because of this, biblical literacy is incredibly important to us.

Each resource we create offers opportunities for children to explore the Bible through multiple learning styles. We want children not only to have fun when our learning materials are in their classrooms, but to have chances to explore and experience the rich stories of our faith. This sets the faith foundation of each child that will continue to be built as he or she grows.

We have created a three-year Scope and Sequence covering 146 stories from the Bible. These stories draw from the list of important Bible passages children will come to know.

DESIGN THINKING

I felt it was important to include in this chapter an overview of the process the children's unit has implemented to create resources—partly because I think it's good for everyone

Deep Blue History, Philosophy, and Theology

to know how our curriculum is created, and partly because it's one of the ways I am living out my call to be a minister. This process is called Design Thinking. It's a way of creating solutions that is based on deep empathy. It recognizes that we are not in a vacuum. Instead, the ministry we do is in direct partnership with the ministry you do, and it creates connections between the UMPH children's team and the children's teams we seek to support.

This graphic helps give an overview of the process we go through as we create new resources and make changes to the quarterly curriculum.

Design Thinking Model

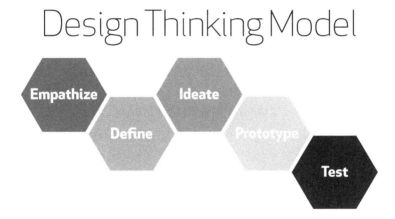

We have been utilizing the Design Thinking process since 2014. Here are our steps:

- We get a randomized list of churches who have purchased children's curriculum from Cokesbury. It does not matter what brand of curriculum a church uses.
- We contact each church to set up an hour-long phone or video call with the children's team.

- On the day of the call, we listen deeply as we ask questions of the person who works with children and families. This person (or persons) could be a pastor, a director of children's ministry, or a volunteer. We ask about a typical week at their church, ask about their passions and frustrations, and ask what we could do to be better partners in ministry. We say a prayer to bless the church, the church's children, and the church's community.
- We look for patterns that emerge from these calls. For instance, every single church we have been in contact with since 2014 has told us they have a hard time getting information to parents and caregivers.
- Once we have identified several patterns, we ideate solutions.
- Then, we test these ideas. Sometimes this is through surveys or follow-up calls. Sometimes it's the creation of a prototype session, and we send the samples to our church partners to try out and give us feedback.
- We tweak the idea to accommodate the feedback we receive.
- Then, we go to market with our products, hoping they help children and their caregivers come to know God.

CLOSING

Everything we do is rooted in this hope—to reach, empower, and equip children, and those who care for them, with grace-based resources that help them on the journey to understand themselves as children of God, explore and deepen their relationships with God through Jesus Christ, and love and serve God and neighbor. We hope to accomplish this task in ministry together. o

② Sacred Conversations

L. J. Zimmerman

> If [the] attitude of patience and humility is right and necessary in every field of education, it is all the more important in the area of religious education where nothing belongs to the adult, neither the soul of the child nor what is being offered to the child. All that is being transmitted belongs to God and is given by God out of God's goodness and for our joy. The child, as a living being, is a being in development. The adult educator is given the privilege of assisting and consciously participating in a creative act; but he or she must not forget that only a part in it is reserved for him or her and not even the principle part.[2]
>
> —Gianna Gobbi, *Listening to God with Children*

DEFINING THE SACRED

Perhaps one of the most important functions of religious education is to create space for sacred conversations with children. This chapter will explore ways to create such space in your own ministry with children. But first, let's take a moment to define sacred conversations. Adults tend to define *sacred* by contrasting it with something else, like *profane* or *ordinary*. The mundane, messy, coarse, and unrefined parts of our daily lives are not typically included in our idea of the sacred. *Sacred* connotes a space set apart from our ordinary

---

2 Gianna Gobbi, *Listening to God with Children* (Loveland, OH: Treehaus Communications, Inc., 1998), 13–14.

lives—a space and time in which we can meet God without the constraints of daily-ness.

As you seek to open up space for sacred conversations with children, this division between the sacred and the ordinary is the first idea to let go. The dividing lines between sacred and profane, holy and ordinary, are learned. Children do not begin putting boundaries around their encounters with the divine until they are taught to do so. In children's innate spiritual lives, there is no distinction between the sacred and the ordinary. Children meet God in ordinary experiences of play, nurture, discovery, wonder, and awe.

Sacred Language

In her book, *Children's Spirituality: What It Is and Why It Matters*, Rebecca Nye traces the language children use to express their sacred experiences. Children's language varies widely in early childhood. As they grow, they are taught the "appropriate" religious language to use in expressing their spiritual experiences.[3] Adults who minister to children understandably want to pass on a shared Christian language to children. However, we must remember that we don't give children spirituality by giving them language for it. Children are already created with the capacity to connect with God and experience God's presence. In sharing our own words for spirituality, we must be careful not to communicate that children's own understanding of their relationship with God is invalid or wrong.

Children's lack of distinction between the sacred and the profane poses an interesting challenge to adults who care for them. How can one tell when one is having a "sacred

---

3 Rebecca Nye, *Children's Spirituality: What It Is and Why It Matters* (London: Church House Publishing, 2009), 27–28.

conversation" at all? Is every conversation sacred? Well, yes and no. The truth is that children process our interactions in ways that surprise even those who know them best. We don't always know when a conversation will have a significant impact on the spirituality of a child. But there are clues to help guide us. The first clue is that children's reality is mediated through stories. Children are naturally narrative theologians, and the stories they hear, tell, and make up on the spot are the heart of sacred conversations.

SACRED STORIES

Even before children are interested in linear narratives, they are constantly making meaning through stories. The characters, symbols, and themes of the biblical and cultural narratives loom large in children's imaginations. For very young children, reality and fantasy intermingle. They aren't typically interested in the logic or plot of the stories, but the characters feel as real to them as friends. As children grow, they become more interested in the narrative arcs, especially the conflicts and resolutions. They tend to become concerned with narrative themes like fairness and love. Stories mediate truth for children; children use stories to explore the deepest truths humans must reckon with—the nature of freedom, love, meaning, and death.

Stealth Theologians

Adults who aren't attuned to the innate spirituality of children often miss these holy moments of exploration. The child who only talks about Batman locking up bad guys might not sound very theological, but might very well be exploring the meaning of justice and freedom. The reality is that most children today have much more exposure to cultural narratives than to biblical narratives. Gone are the days when children learned to read using the Bible and when cultural discourses were steeped in biblical references. When children arrive in Sunday school, they are already shaped by powerful cultural and familial stories. When children learn a new story, they filter it through their existing categories and narrative frameworks. Once, I told the Bible story of Zacchaeus to a group of children. Later, I observed a four-year-old boy retell the story to himself. In his version, Zacchaeus was a "bad guy" and Jesus rightfully put Zacchaeus in jail. Despite the fact that I had told the Bible story moments before, the cultural narrative of "good guys," "bad guys," and "criminal justice" were already so powerful that the Bible story was seamlessly altered in this boy's mind. I reminded the boy that Jesus invited himself over to Zacchaeus's house for dinner, and we wondered together about why Jesus behaved in such a radically different way. If we let them, Bible stories can open up profound conversations about our cultural narratives.

Breaking Open the Bible
Sacred conversations with children are about opening up the conversation between biblical narratives and cultural narratives. Why do we still tell our stories? What difference do they make? What new perspective do they offer? We make space for sacred conversations when we invite children to enter the biblical narratives on their own terms—they can even bring Batman. We make space for sacred conversations when we resist the urge to teach the "moral of the story," effectively ending the conversation before it's begun. We make space for sacred conversations when we use our imaginations to fill in gaps in the narratives, and invite children to do the same. When we break the biblical stories open, they become living words, able to bring us closer to God and to one another.

A common resistance people feel when they consider breaking open the biblical narratives is fear. What if we end up with the wrong interpretation? How can we alter the narratives of Scripture by using our imagination? The short answer to these fears is: Don't worry. We can't break the Bible. It's the living Word of God, passed down to us through generations. God is present with us when we read it and seek to hear God's voice through its stories. The long response is: Have you ever heard of midrash? Let me tell you about it. . . .

What We Can Learn from Midrash

Midrash is a centuries-old form of interpretation practiced by Jewish rabbis. Midrashic writings creatively engage the text of the Hebrew Bible, filling in gaps, considering the stories from alternate points of view, and harmonizing contradictions. Midrash often explores ethical and theological questions invoked by the stories, and often addresses burning moral questions of the author's historical moment. Midrashic interpretation enlivens the stories and allows them to speak anew in the present moment.

The *Midrash,* with a capital *M,* refers to specific collections of midrashic writings, typically from the first ten centuries of the Common Era. Famous rabbis' midrashic writings have been preserved over time, even (or especially) when rabbis disagree with one another. Midrash isn't meant to be a final word; it's part of a faith-filled conversation.

Midrash isn't just an ancient form of interpretation, limited to early rabbis. Plenty of modern people practice midrashic interpretation. Midrashic children's books are available, such as *Does God Have a Big Toe? Stories About Stories in the Bible* by Rabbi Marc Gellman. Christians have been inspired by their Jewish neighbors to practice this creative form of interpretation.

The good news is, you don't have to give your children a history lesson in rabbinic Judaism to practice midrash with them. Just start incorporating creative wondering time into your lessons. Wondering time invites children to perform their own midrash by using their imaginations to enter the story. You've probably already used some of these midrashic interpretation techniques in your lessons without even knowing it!

TIPS FOR WONDERING TIME

Here are a few ideas that can help break open the Bible stories and spark children's theological imagination.

- **Ask playful, open-ended wonder questions that invite the children into the story.** Don't be alarmed if your questions are met by silence. Silence doesn't necessarily signify disinterest or misunderstanding; it can also signal nonverbal processing and timidness. If you start to feel uncomfortable in the silence, slowly count to ten in your mind before you ask a follow-up question.

- **Don't dismiss even zany answers!** Children sometimes offer zany or borderline inappropriate responses to get attention. Other times, those weird responses are their honest-to-goodness reflections on the story. The best way to diffuse the attention-seekers and honor the honest answers is to take every response seriously.

- **Avoid making judgments about the children's responses, even positive ones.** Children can tell in your words and body language if you're looking for a particular response and it's not the one they gave. Approach wonder conversations without any end-goal in mind, and an openness to considering new ideas. If possible, respond to the children's responses with more wonder questions. rather than statements.

- Invite the children to consider the story from various characters' perspectives, especially traditionally silent characters such as women, people with disabilities, or "enemy" characters like the robbers in the parable of the good Samaritan. Wonder aloud how they might feel and what they might say about God or Jesus. You can even include animals and inanimate objects in this exercise!

- Notice gaps or unanswered questions in the story, and point them out to the children. For example, no explanation is given for why an angel/God wrestles Jacob in the middle of the night. Invite children to wonder about this confusing scene and share their explanations.

- Respect children's urge to process the stories through the lens of their cultural narratives. Don't take offense if children wonder aloud whether Jesus is a zombie or draw Noah in a spaceship rather than an ark. These are not signs of children's failure to take the Bible seriously. They are signs that the children are engaged in the stories and attempting to integrate them into their narrative world.

- Encourage the children when they ask ethical or theological questions about biblical narratives, even when they are difficult. If it occurs to a child that God allowed all the humans except for Noah to drown, try to avoid glossing over the question or shying away from its implications. It's okay to admit that you don't have all the answers, and to affirm that there are difficult parts of the Bible stories.

- **Encourage children to imagine various endings to a story.** Use prompts such as, "What if this character had made a different choice?" For example, once I had a group of children acting out the story of Moses. Two second-grade children played Egyptian soldiers. They stopped in the middle of the drama and announced that they didn't want to be mean to the Hebrew families. As a group, we talked through the options available to the Egyptian soldiers. They decided to imagine what would happen if some of the Egyptian soldiers decided to help the Hebrew slaves escape. The drama transformed from a recitation of lines to a conversation about power and moral responsibility.

- **If the story is confusing or not entirely clear, resist the urge to explain it,** or even to retell it in a way that you find more clear. It's best to stick as closely to the biblical text as is age-appropriate for these types of stories. Parables are prime targets for well-intentioned retellings that zap the mystery right out of the story. Consider the fact that Jesus' teachings largely took the form of parables for a reason. The wild mystery of parables was preserved so that each person can wonder anew. A creative retelling may offer a new perspective, but sometimes it can take away the children's opportunity to make their own creative meaning from the story.

- **When children express their boredom, offer them a creative challenge.** Even the most thoughtfully structured wondering time is vulnerable to the depressing response, "I'm bored! I've heard this story before!" Rather than cringing, congratulate them. If they know the story well enough to be bored, they are ready to be creative! Midrash is the work of people who know the Bible like the back of their hands. Boredom, especially in older children, is a sign that they are ready for more creative midrashic work. Encourage them to make a comic book that tells the story from a different point of view or write a modern retelling to present to the group. Have them make a children's book to read to younger children or draw the story as if they were one of the characters. In other words, make it a challenge for them to find new meaning in the sacred stories.

These are simply a few ideas to get you started. As you continue to break open the Bible stories with your children, you'll discover that this approach to the Bible is more of an ethos than a method.

FOLLOWING UP

As children grow comfortable digging into Scripture together, be prepared for them to begin connecting the Bible with their daily life naturally. The power of Bible stories is that they continue to speak into our lives, if we let them—even the difficult parts. Be prepared to offer pastoral care to children who face conflict in the home, bullying at school, divorce and parental separation, and other adverse experiences. Sacred conversations about Scripture can segue quickly into sacred conversations about life.

It's often a good idea to follow a wondering conversation with a response activity that allows for some individualized work. This gives you an opportunity to follow up one-on-one or in small groups with students who may be processing the story on a deeper level. And, of course, abide by your Safe Sanctuaries Policy with regard to any disclosures made by the children.

After an individual response time, it's helpful to bring the group back together for a time of prayer, worship, and blessing. Sacred conversations bring up reflection and meaning-making, and our ultimate goal is to bring that holy work to God. Prayer and worship are our response to the deep truths we discover in the sacred stories.

As you approach the holy work of sacred conversations with children, remember that God is with you. The Holy Spirit gives creative energy to these conversations and uses them in ways we can't imagine in the lives of children. May we approach this blessing and responsibility with awe and wonder. o

③ Using
Deep Blue Resources

Daphna Flegal

These curriculum resources started with you! We talked to many of you and heard your priorities. In response, we are continuously seeking to develop new and meaningful resources just for you!

We want to offer biblically solid, theologically sound, age-graded, and age-appropriate learning tools that are easy to use, fun for children, easy to teach, and filled with options.

Deep Blue: Teaching with Confidence

NURSERY

This resource has been specially written for children from birth through 35 months and those who care for them.

We believe that for these little ones, curriculum is everything they experience from the time they enter the church doors until the time they are picked up.

Our number one reason for creating this curriculum is so that you can begin to speak faith and blessing to each child.

Activity Centers

Each month your little bitties will experience one Bible story through playing, singing, and interacting. At the start of each month, set up the monthly centers. These are

- Art Activity Center
- Pretend Play Activity Center
- Sensory Activity Center
- Special unit-specific Activity Center

Sensory Activity

Before class: Gather craft sto green chenille stems into 1-in of this activity.

- Encourage the children to

Each week your children will begin by playing in these centers. Then, you'll sing the unit song, and hear and experience the unit's story. There is a new activity for creating, playing, and blessing in each session. Be sure to send home the weekly Bible Story Picture Card to continue the learning at home.

Using Deep Blue Resources

PRESCHOOL

Developed for children ages 3–4. Resources for this age level include:

Leader Guide

- Lessons are easy to lead, fast to prepare, biblically grounded, educationally sound, flexible, and fun!
- 13 session guides include reproducible activity sheets, Bible verses, games, art, science, worship, prayers, and more.

Bible Story Sheets

- Colorful storybook pages share a different Bible story each week.
- Simple words and colorful pictures engage children and help them gain a deeper understanding of each Bible story.
- Ideas allow parents and caregivers to continue the learning at home.
- Stickers go along with each session.

Deep Blue: Teaching with Confidence

Activity Sheets

- 13 easy crafts offer a creative outlet while reinforcing the Bible stories.
- Self-directed activities develop preschoolers' independent learning.
- Faith Family Activities encourage families to experience aspects of each Bible story together throughout the week.

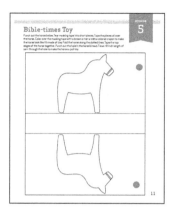

Class Kit

- Large (11-by-17), colorful posters enhance the Bible story.
- Includes games, storytelling figures, cards, and a colorful attendance chart.

Using Deep Blue Resources

EARLY ELEMENTARY

Developed for children ages 5–6. Resources for this age level include:

Leader Guide
- Lessons are easy to lead, fast to prepare, biblically grounded, educationally sound, flexible, and fun!
- 13 session guides include reproducible activity sheets, Bible verses, games, art, science, worship, prayers, and more.

Bible Story Sheets
- 13 Bible stories use colorful pictures and simple words that children and their caregivers can read together.
- Stories are written on an early-elementary grade level to help children engage in the Bible story, learn to love reading, and enjoy spending time with parents and caregivers.
- Faith Family Activities encourage families to experience aspects of each Bible story together throughout the week.

Activity Sheets
- 13 ready-to-go activities offer a creative outlet while reinforcing the Bible story.
- Activities are simple to prepare and easy to teach for busy volunteers and teachers.

Class Kit
- Large (11-by-17), colorful posters enhance the Bible story.
- Includes games, storytelling figures, cards, and a colorful attendance chart.

Deep Blue: Teaching with Confidence

MIDDLE AND OLDER ELEMENTARY

Developed for children ages 7–8 and 9–10. Resources for these age levels include:

Leader Guide
- Lessons are easy to lead, fast to prepare, biblically grounded, educationally sound, flexible, and fun!
- 13 session guides include reproducible activity sheets, Bible verses, games, art, science, worship, prayers, and more.

Bible Story Sheets
- 13 sheets, one for each session, present an interactive Bible story, faith development, spiritual practices, and ideas for families.

Activity Sheets
- 13–15 puzzles and journal pages relate to the Bible message.

Class Kit
- Large (11-by-17), colorful posters enhance the Bible story, mission experience, and more.

Using Deep Blue Resources

FOR PRESCHOOL THROUGH OLDER ELEMENTARY

Digital Resources
- Downloadable Leader Guides for all ages are editable files for customizing each session to fit your class and congregational needs
- A new curriculum builder to customize your church's Scope and Sequence
- Online subscriptions which give access to the editable Leader Guides, Rotation Stations, and Deep Blue Life

Adventure DVD
The Adventure DVD contains

- 13 episodes that tell the Bible story in 3-D and 2-D animation,
- monthly Bible verse videos that help the children learn the Bible verses,
- four music videos with music written by award-winning musician Dennis Scott, and
- a unit Bible trivia quiz to review each quarter's Bible stories with the children.

Deep Blue Annual Music CD
The official *Deep Blue Annual Music CD* contains 13 songs that support the stories taught in Deep Blue.

Deep Blue Apps

The Deep Blue Adventures App includes a parent dashboard that is updated weekly to include the Adventure video. It also includes fun Scripture memory games that children can play at home.

The Deep Blue Bible Storybook App is a companion to the *Deep Blue Bible Storybook*. Use the app to scan a Bible story, and watch the corresponding video. Both apps are available in iOS and Android app stores.

deepbluekids.com

Find teacher helps, parent helps, training videos, extra coloring sheets, and more—all free at our website!

CEB Deep Blue Kids Bible

This engaging, interactive Bible offers four-color icons and illustrations throughout with a wealth of notes, devotionals, Bible facts, and other interactive elements to capture inquisitive young minds. Plus, the *CEB Deep Blue Kids Bible* will encourage a thirst for God's timeless message as young readers join three lifelike kids in discovering the Bible and what it means to their lives.

Using Deep Blue Resources

Deep Blue Bible Storybook

The *Deep Blue Bible Storybook* tells 146 Bible stories in a way young children understand. It has fun, bright illustrations sure to captivate! The Bible Storybook is organized in a way that helps children begin to learn the books of the Bible and practice beginning Bible skills. Plus, there are tips for adults, wonder questions to help children experience the story, and prayers and songs to deepen the faith of the young child.

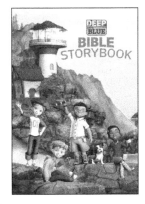

Deep Blue Kids Bible Dictionary

Make reading the Bible a little easier for your 7- to 12-year-old children with the *Deep Blue Kids Bible Dictionary*. They'll not only learn the pronunciation and meaning of names, places, and events, but colorful artwork will help them better understand the activities, occupations, and living conditions of those who lived in Bible times.

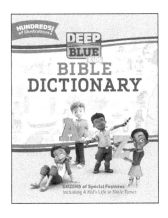

Deep Blue: Teaching with Confidence

SUBMERGE: DEEP BLUE FOR TWEENS

Developed for students ages 10–12 as a way to prepare your tweens to transition to youth group. Submerge encourages tweens to dig deeper into the Bible, ask tough questions, and creatively engage their faith. Resources for this age level include:

Leader Guide

- Flexible and easy-to-use session guides that are biblically grounded and engaging. Includes a Bible Improv Script for each lesson.

SUBMERGE Magazine

- Articles encourage tweens to make meaningful connections among the Bible, faith, and their everyday lives.
- Prompts encourage thoughtful reflection and discussion.

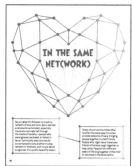

Diver's Log

- Weekly prompts encourage creative thinking and playful reflection on the Bible story.
- Includes prayer pages.

_ _ _ _ _ Using Deep Blue Resources _ _ _ _

ONE ROOM SUNDAY SCHOOL

Deep Blue One Room Sunday School is ideal for churches where children of various ages learn together as a group. Everything needed for Sunday school is included in one convenient kit for children ages 3–12. These sessions can also be used for a second Sunday school hour, Wednesday night, or an after-school program. Provides a three-year Bible overview.

The One Room Sunday School Kit contains a Leader Guide, Reproducible Kids' Book, Resource Pack, CD-ROM, and Deep Blue Kids Tote.

The CD-ROM is a quarterly music CD-ROM with added PowerPoint slides, song sheets, and instrumental tracks.

The Resource Pack contains colorful, easy-to-use posters to reinforce the Bible story, plus storytelling helps, an attendance chart, and more!

The Reproducible Kids' Book is 96 pages of activities tailored to each session throughout the quarter. From puzzles to creative-writing prompts, this resource will lead children to a deeper understanding of each Bible lesson.

_ _ _ _ Deep Blue: Teaching with Confidence _ _ _ _

LARGE GROUP/SMALL GROUP

Children gather in large groups for the Bible story, music and movement, and more. They break into age-level small groups to dig deeper and apply the story to their daily lives. This resource is perfect for Sunday school, children's church, and midweek sessions.

The Large Group/Small Group Kit includes: Leader Guide, CD-ROM, and Adventure DVD.

The Leader Guide includes 13 step-by-step session guides, reproducible sheets for large-group and small-group activities, and interactive Bible stories.

The CD-ROM contains music (instrumental tracks and vocal tracks), PowerPoints with Bible story graphics, song sheets, and PDFs of the Leader Guide.

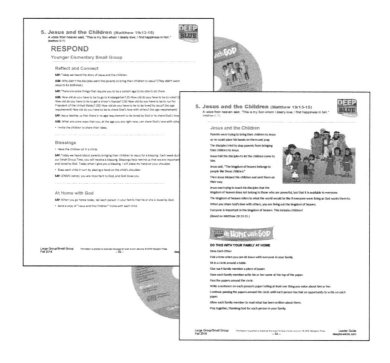

Using Deep Blue Resources

ROTATION STATIONS

Through the new Deep Blue rotation-model curriculum, children will experience the Bible story in many different ways. As a result, each Bible story and its meaning will stay with them for life!

Through art, cooking, games, missions, science, spiritual practices, and storytelling and drama, children will explore Bible stories. Children will have opportunities to be creative and give thanks for all the great things God is doing. Each unit includes teacher helps and a parent resource.

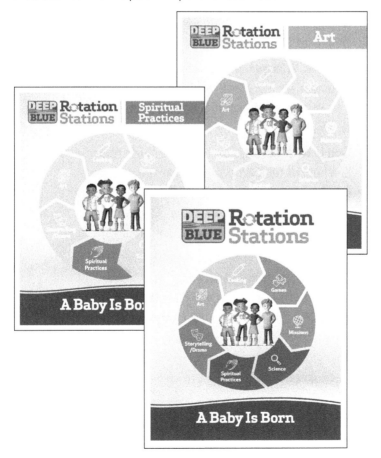

DEEP BLUE LIFE

Deep Blue Life is a downloadable, customizable curriculum option that focuses on living life faithfully. Through Bible stories, stories about faith leaders, and spiritual practices, your children will be empowered to take part in God's great story!

Choose from these session categories:

- **Spiritual Practices:** sessions that help children form habits that connect them with God (such as Silence, Prayer, Unplugging, Worship, Sharing Meals, and Baptism)

- **Cloud of Witnesses:** sessions about our faith leaders (such as Francis of Assisi, John Wesley, Harriet Tubman, Dietrich Bonhoeffer, and Ruby Bridges)

- **God Is with Us:** sessions about real-life topics and how to see God even when life seems hard (such as When We Are Bullied, When We're Really Angry, When Someone We Love Dies, When We're Fighting with Our Friends or Siblings)

- **Faith and Culture:** sessions about how to remain faithful when culture influences us (such as Media Myths—I have to look like the people I see on TV; Anti-Racism—curiosity and empathy; Who Is My Neighbor?—the hungry and thirsty)

④ How to Set Up
a Deep Blue Classroom

Erin R. Floyd

Intentionality is key to creating a meaningful space for children to learn and grow. Designing an intentional space means considering what enriches the learning experience and the faith development of each child. Creating intentional space and valuing the learning environment explicitly and implicitly offers children a sense of welcome and belonging to their space and to their faith community.

TAKE A LOOK

Begin by evaluating your space. Notice if the room is child-friendly, age-appropriate, and accessible for all children. Consider using the classroom evaluation found on page 48. Use this as a guide to evaluate your classrooms and children's ministry settings.

Both the environment and the learning materials for the session are active participants in the educational space. Gather appropriate supplies and objects that children are comfortable using. Consider what things are child-friendly and what supplies children ask for. Make these things easy for the children to access.

Consider signage inside and outside the classroom. Outside the classroom, make it clear who meets in the provided space. Consider letting children name their classroom. Post a sign with the name outside. Signs also help visitors. Consider adding age levels or who's included to your classroom signs.

Inside the classroom, take time to make labels. Labeling supplies, cabinets, and shelving helps children know where things belong and where to return used materials. Educational posters and images help make the room inviting and can also be used as educational tools. Consider hanging up Deep Blue posters to match the curriculum being used. Deep Blue posters display an array of diversity and theologically sound images and design. These posters can be found in the individual Class Kits and are created to be age-appropriate.

Now, evaluate how the overall space appears. Is the space overwhelming or overstimulating? Sometimes wall colors or lights are too bright. This especially affects children who have sensory concerns. You might consider using lamps rather than fluorescent lighting and painting the walls a calming color. This also makes the room more inviting.

It is also important to consider the cleanliness and organization of the Sunday school space. A clean and organized space enriches the learning environment. Chaos and clutter interfere with children's ability to participate in the lesson and the learning experience.

INVOLVING OTHERS

An effective and organized space is not possible unless volunteers and children are committed to maintaining the space. Let the children help. Teach children to care about their classroom. Give them jobs such as stacking chairs, putting away supplies, and wiping down the tables. In doing this, children will begin to take ownership of their space.

You might also consider training volunteers and parents to better understand why an intentional classroom is important. Help them understand that children need security, predictability, and cleanliness. These things help everyone thrive and allow for more time to be spent on meaningful relationships, wonder and awe, and overall faith development.

WHAT DOES A DEEP BLUE CLASSROOM LOOK LIKE?

So you might be wondering, what does a Deep Blue classroom actually look like? Ideally, not only is the space inviting and organized, it is also set up in such a way that children can easily engage in the flow of a lesson. See page 47 for a helpful layout of a Deep Blue classroom. Classroom spaces are adaptable and can be altered to best fit your space and your children.

Begin by having a central gathering and worship space. You might choose to place a rug in this area for children to gather and sit. A small table would also be appropriate. On the table, you could place things, such as liturgical symbols and colors, a Deep Blue Kids Bible, and possibly a candle or candles. Regularly, you might switch out the table coverings to match the liturgical season or the Bible story.

Next, think about your choice in furniture. Consider where the children sit to do their work and play. If they sit at tables, are the tables and chairs appropriate size for the age of the children? Is there space to move around, or is the room overly crowded? Children need creative space to wiggle, move, and play. The Sunday school space also needs to be accessible for all children. Take into consideration children with differing abilities. Can all children feel welcomed in your space?

Make room for shelving or cabinets that hold supplies. Make sure child-friendly supplies are accessible to children. A bookshelf or children's library would also be appropriate. Fill the bookshelves with Bibles and books that relate to the liturgical season, draw upon Bible stories, or connect to other things going on in your congregation and the world. Books are a great way for children to do some independent learning and make connections between the Bible and everyday life.

Also, make space to display art. Are there places for artwork to dry, be displayed, or stay safe during the week? Consider hanging string or wire across the wall to attach art with clothespins or other hanging devices. You can also place empty frames on the wall to fill with children's work. Make something that is easy to change out regularly and easy for children to help with. By displaying children's artwork, you are helping children feel included in the classroom.

How to Set Up a Deep Blue Classroom

RECYCLED SUPPLIES

We strive to write sessions that require only affordable, easy-to-find supplies. There are sometimes special supplies required for an activity, but these can be found at most craft stores. However, sometimes budgets do not allow everyone to buy brand-new and top-of-the-line supplies. Still, it is possible to have great supplies with things you already own. You can ask your congregation for specific things, such as unwanted magazines, extra fabric, empty plastic containers, crayons, markers, and colored pencils. Reuse and recycle materials. Look around your church for supplies that are no longer being used. So many things can be used as craft and art supplies.

One suggestion is to use dried-up markers to make watercolors. Take a jar or spray bottle filled with water. Place the markers, tips down, in the water and let them sit overnight. The next day you will have colored paint. It works even better if you remove the felt tips from the plastic holders and put them in the bottle. Finding ways to upcyle resources helps save money and also teaches kids about the importance of reusing and caring how we use our resources.

MEDIA IN THE CLASSROOM

It is important to consider what kind of media to include in the classroom. Deep Blue curriculum strives to help children transition from their everyday lives into the sacred  learning environment. Technology is changing rapidly, and children are exposed to technology and media from an early age. The Deep Blue team has considered thoughtful ways to effectively incorporate technology in the classroom. However, this may vary for different congregations. Deep Blue sessions do not rely on technology, but rather use it to enhance the overall classroom experience. Many classrooms today have televisions, iPads, and computers. Other technology can often be used as a connection point to engage the world beyond the Sunday school room and dive deeper into the overall lesson.

Therefore, it is OK to include a television or computer inside the Sunday school classroom. It is also appropriate to not do this. It's about being strategic and finding a balance. It is difficult to find ways to create a reflective and spiritual experience for children while also meeting students where they are. The *Deep Blue Adventure DVD* provides short videos that help bring the Bible story to life but also offer reflective and thought-provoking questions. Technology has its place, but so does engaging with one another and spending time with God. Deep Blue tries to honor both.

If you decide to use technology, consider letting older children help operate the devices. This is a great way to include them in leadership and for older children to feel involved. You can also consider a television cabinet or a television on a cart. This way, you can put away the technology when it is not being used and it will not serve as a distraction.

QUIET SPACE

Sometimes children need a quiet area to reflect, calm down, or just be alone. It is a great idea to create this space inside or near your classroom. Consider using a tent, pillows, books, and quiet toys. Sometimes children need a place to go to feel safe and secure when they are upset or feeling overwhelmed. Consider having a volunteer or staff person be responsible for comforting children in the quiet space. This should be someone with a calming presence and someone who understands children's wants and needs. Quiet spaces are a great way to help any child have personal time to better understand themselves and to sit quietly in a sometimes overstimulating world.

WHERE TO START?

Much of this might seem overwhelming, and you might be wondering where to start. Begin by slowly implementing changes. Consider using the evaluation found on page 48. What small changes can you make? Take time to simply clean out and clean up the space. Involve your children, parents, and volunteers. Having support from others makes the task less daunting. Hold a cleanup day where people of all ages can help create a more intentional space for your children's ministry.

SHARED SPACE

We also recognize that not all churches have their own classrooms and children's ministry spaces. You might be wondering how to adapt or apply this information to a shared church space.

First, consider items easy to remove from the space, such as lightweight tables, rolling carts, and laminated posters that can easily come off the wall. Also, maintain a space to easily hold your own supplies.

Be collaborative and find ways all users of the shared space can claim it as their own in unique ways. Compromise and share items, such as tables and chairs, technology, and decor. Have good communication with everyone who shares the space. Make sure all parties involved are willing to cooperate and respect one another's individual areas, supplies, and structure.

Consider charts or posters on the wall that demonstrate how the room should be set up and organized for each group sharing the space. When one group leaves the space, they can refer to the chart to make sure things are arranged appropriately.

Keep it clean. Make sure you clean up after yourselves and others do the same. It might seem silly, but remember the Girl Scouts rule, "Always leave a space cleaner than you found it." This is a simple way to show respect to those who are also using the shared space.

Keep it organized. Make it easy on yourself to arrange, set up, and take down your class setting. Maybe claim certain places within the room that can be your own, or have a closet nearby where your things can be stored. Consider having help doing your setup and cleanup. A team of volunteers might simplify the process.

It is possible to have an intentional space and a shared space. It just has to be done carefully and collaboratively. It will be challenging, but it will likely help you be more organized and purposeful in the ways you choose to navigate your classroom space. O

How to Set Up a Deep Blue Classroom

CLASSROOM LAYOUT

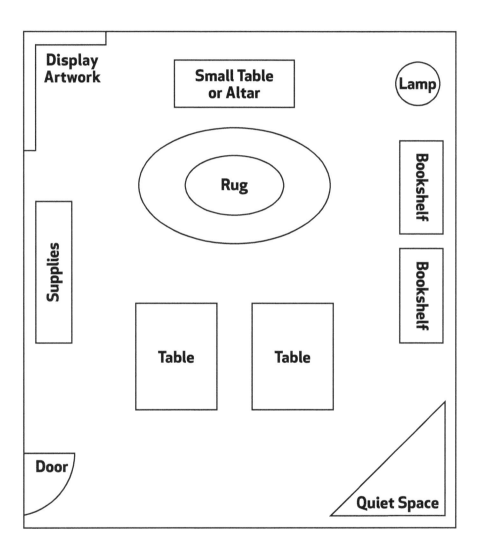

Deep Blue: Teaching with Confidence

CLASSROOM EVALUATION

- As you approach the classroom, can you tell who meets there?

- As you enter the room, what is the first thing you notice?

- Is there something that makes you want to come into the room? If so, what?

- Can you tell this is a Sunday school space?

- Is the room too light? too dark?

- Is the space too crowded? too empty?

- Is the furniture child-friendly?

- Are things accessible for all children?

- Are outlets covered and protected?

⑤ The Flow
of a Deep Blue Session

Daphna Flegal

Each Deep Blue session plan is designed to make it easy for you to teach and implement the lesson with children. The first thing you will want to look at is the first page of the session plan. At the top of the page is the heading and the Bible verse. The heading tells you what the Bible story is for the session. The Bible verse is directly underneath the heading. This verse will be the same for the four to five weeks in the unit or month. The heading and Bible verse appear at the top of each page so you'll have an easy reference.

> **5. Jesus and the Children** (Matthew 19:13-15)
> A voice from heaven said, "This is my Son whom I dearly love; I find happiness in him." Matthew 3:17

PLAN

The next part of the page is PLAN. This gives you the session outline and the supplies you will need for the activities. Basic supplies are listed separately. These are the supplies you'll most likely find in your church—crayons, construction paper, glue, pencils,

> **PLAN**
>
> **Session Outline**
> **1. Gather**
> Greeting
> Bible-times Toy
> Act Out the Story
> Transition to Explore
>
> **2. Explore**
> Sacred Conversations
> Hear and See the Bible Story

Deep Blue: Teaching with Confidence

and so forth. Also included in basic supplies is the *CEB Deep Blue Kids Bible* (for all ages) and the *Deep Blue Bible Storybook* (for Preschool, Early Elementary, and occasionally, Middle Elementary). Additional supplies that you might not easily find in the church closet are listed under each section.

Before You Teach

Included on this first page is "Before You Teach." This is a short explanation of the Bible story for the session. It contains information about biblical interpretation and biblical customs that relate to the Bible story and its meaning for children.

> **Before You Teach**
>
> In today's lesson, we'll explore the far disciples tried to keep the children fr something. Help your children think ab something (even if there is a good reas the children must have felt when they
>
> When the disciples discouraged the par weren't intentionally being mean to the social norms and expectations of the ti persons in their own right. Children we

Use the information on this first page to get yourself and your room ready for the children you will teach. Take the time to make the room inviting, and be ready to greet the children as they arrive.

The Flow of a Deep Blue Session

GATHER

As the children enter your space, you will use the suggested activities from GATHER. It's important to greet each and every child. You may want to start a greeting tradition. You can welcome each child with a special handshake. Ask the child what kind of handshake he or she would like. You might give the child a high five or a fist bump, or use your finger to draw a smiley face on the back of the child's hand. You could also say a special greeting or establish a short greeting song. The idea is to let each child know you are glad she or he is here. You may also want to add words of affirmation to each greeting. These greeting traditions help build trusting relationships with the children you teach and affirm each child as an important member of the family of God.

> **GATHER**
>
> **Greeting**
> *Before class: Display the Attendan[ce]*
> - Play, "Tell Me the Stories of Jes[us]" ritual.
> - Show the children where to pla[ce]
> - Help each child put a Jesus and [...]
>
> **SAY:** Today our Bible story is abou[t] ages are important in God's famil[y]

Deep Blue: Teaching with Confidence

After your greeting, show the children where to place their offerings and mark their attendance. There is an attendance chart in the Class Kit for each age level. The Preschool Bible Story Sheets include attendance stickers that relate to the day's Bible story and offer an opportunity to begin talking about the Bible story with each child. For Early Elementary through Older Elementary, let the children mark the chart with a marker or crayon, or provide generic stickers.

> **A—Bible-times Toy (Activity**
> *Before class: Punch out "Bible-times Toy" (Activit*
> - Help each child follow the directions to make
>
> **SAY:** Children in Bible times played with toy anim
>
> ———————— OR ————————
>
> **B—Act Out the Story (Drama)**
> *Before class: Set up an area of your room with B*
> - Invite the children to dress up in Bible-times c
> - Choose a child to be Jesus. Have Jesus stand a
> - Encourage the children to wrap the dolls in bla
>
> **SAY:** Stop! Jesus does not have time for children

Now it's time to introduce the Bible story. In Deep Blue Connects, you have two options to choose from at this point in the session. You may choose one of the options or, if your time permits, do both. It's up to you. You know what your children enjoy.

This section ends with a transition to the Bible story circle or area. Transitions are important to the flow of any session. Give the children at least a five-minute warning for transition time. For older ages, we suggest a bell you can ring. This allows the children to anticipate when it's time to switch gears and move to a different part of the session. Involve the children in cleanup. Then move them to the story area. For preschoolers, this is usually some kind of movement, like tiptoeing or marching. Transitions help cut down on chaos and actually provide security for the children. When they hear the bell or the cleanup song, they know what to do.

_ _ _ _ _ The Flow of a Deep Blue Session _ _ _ _

EXPLORE

Now you and the children are together and ready to explore the day's Bible story. This section begins with "Sacred Conversations." This is a time to talk with your children, asking about their week, their feelings, and their lives. Talking and LISTENING to your children helps them feel important and that they belong. If everyone wants to talk at once, you may want to use a talking stick (or other object) during this time. Only the person holding the talking stick gets to talk—everyone else must listen. Assure the children that everyone will have a turn with the talking stick.

EXPLORE

Sacred Conversations

- Have the children sit down in your story area and put their toys away.

ASK: I wonder,
- how do you feel today? Are you happy? Are you sad?
- what's the best thing that happened today?
- what's one thing you're thankful for?

Deep Blue: Teaching with Confidence

After "Sacred Conversations," it's time to "Hear and See the Bible Story." You can read the story to the children from the *Deep Blue Bible Storybook* or have the children read the story directly from the *CEB Deep Blue Kids Bible*. Using these two resources helps the children learn to navigate the Bible for themselves. Next, enjoy seeing the Bible story on the *Deep Blue Adventure DVD*. This is a video of the Bible story told with animated characters. In the DVD, your children will meet the Deep Blue Kids—Kat, Caleb, Asia, and Edgar—and their families. At the end of the video, one of the characters will ask your children a wondering question. Spend a few minutes encouraging your children to respond.

Following "Hear and See the Bible Story" is "Interact with the Bible Story." You will find this part of the session in the Bible Story Sheets. This is a retelling of the Bible story that involves the children. For older children, this might be a play they can read and act out. For younger children, it might be motions they can do as the teacher reads the story to them.

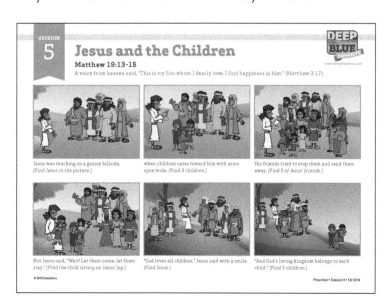

----- The Flow of a Deep Blue Session -----

These activities give you the opportunity to present the Bible story to your children in different ways. Some children may prefer reading the Bible for themselves; others may prefer seeing the animated story; still others may prefer moving to and acting out the story. Every child is different. Allow them to encounter the Bible story in the ways they like best.

After the Bible story, we suggest that you teach the children the Bible verse. Since we have the same Bible verse for the whole month, your children have the opportunity to learn the verse without the pressure of memorization. You can find signs from American Sign Language (ASL) for each verse in your resources. Signing is a way to involve the children in movement with the verse, and that helps memory. While we use ASL signs with Bible verses, the signs are not actual translations of the verse into ASL. ASL is a language all its own. We are simply borrowing signs for individual words.

Now it's time for another transition. The children will move to activities that give them the opportunity to respond to the Bible story.

RESPOND

Once again, you have two activities you may choose from. You can do one or both, depending on your time and children. These activities will often include a game and an art option. If you're only going to do one, choose an activity based on your children's interest.

Spend part of your session with "Missions." These activities will be different each week, but will continue in each year. This is where your children will make connections from the Bible story to ways they can serve the church, the community, and the world.

End this section of the session with the final transition to BLESS.

RESPOND

A—Stop and Go (Game)

- Have the children move to an open area of the room.
- Play, "Tell Me the Stories of Jesus" (Adventure DVD), or sing, "Jesus Loves M[e]
- Encourage the children to move to the music.

SAY: Stop! Don't bother Jesus!

- Stop the music and have the children freeze (stop moving).

SAY: Go! Jesus wants to see you!

- Start the music and play the game again.

---OR---

B—Heart Prints (Art)

Before class: Photocopy "Heart Prints" (Leader Guide—p. 36) for each child.

- Show the children how to color a thumb with a watercolor marker and then inside the heart to make prints. Encourage the children to fill their hearts w[ith]
- Use hand wipes to clean the children's thumbs.

SAY: Each of us has different thumbprints, and each of us is an important part

The Flow of a Deep Blue Session

BLESS

Gather your children together for a time of praise and prayer. Play the theme song, "Deep Blue Family," on the DVD. Let the children interact with the session's Bible mural found in the Class Kit and review the Bible story.

"Praising" time is just that: a time to sing, dance, and speak praises to God. Preschoolers have song cards in the Class Kit that give visual reminders of different songs. Let the children select which songs they want to sing by choosing one of the cards.

The final activity for the session is "Blessing." Go to each child and give a simple blessing. You might use unscented lip balm to draw a heart or cross on the back of each child's hand; have each child dip his or her fingers in a bowl of water; or simply touch each child on a shoulder. Give all the children the message that God loves them and they belong to God's family.

BLESS

Inviting
Before class: Post "Bible M
- Play the song, "Deep Blu
- Gather the children arou (Class Kit—p. 28) to the

PRAY: Thank you, God, for family. Amen.

Praising
Before class: Cut out "Song
- Show the children the so
- Choose one child to pick
- Sing the song on that ca

PRAY: Dear God, thank you

TIP: *If time permits, let the*

Blessing
Before class: Fill a bowl wit
- Show how to gently dip into the bowl.
- One at a time, invite a ch
- Dry the child's hand with

SAY: *(Child's name),* you ar

PRAY: Dear God, thank you

Deep Blue: Teaching with Confidence

Say goodbye as the children leave, and ask them to think about what they can tell their families about today's session. Be sure to give each child the Bible Story Sheet for the day. The back of each sheet suggests activities that families can do together to continue the Bible message at home.

The Flow of a Deep Blue Session

WHEN IT'S OVER...

Breathe deeply. Take a few moments to think through the session. Ask yourself and your co-leader or helper:

How did the children show that they understood the main idea of the session?

How did the children interact with the Bible story?

What did the children really enjoy?

What did not interest the children?

What would you change?

What would you do again?

Look ahead to next week's session (if you will be teaching next week). Identify the next session's Bible story and spend some time allowing its message to inspire you. Say a thank-you prayer. Thank God for the children you teach.

TEN TIPS TO MAKE IT EVEN EASIER

1. Pray.

2. Look over and plan your session before you get to your class.

3. Make the room look inviting (and clean).

4. Greet the children at the door and involve them immediately in the session.

5. If you have children who arrive early, involve them in helping you set up the room.

6. Give a five-minute warning when it's time to move to a new activity.

7. Give your children leadership roles. Preschoolers can be line leaders to help the children move to the story area. Older children can read the Bible story out loud.

Always be sure to ask for volunteers. If a child doesn't want to read aloud, let the child pass.

8. Familiarize yourself with the video equipment. You can quickly lose the children's attention if you're looking in all the cabinets for the remote.

9. Check for allergies before serving snacks.

10. Always have two adults in the room. This is a Safe Sanctuary rule and provides safety for all persons involved. o

⑥ Deep Blue
Teacher Tips

Laura Allison

> Then Jesus called them to him and said, "Allow the children to come to me. Don't forbid them, because God's kingdom belongs to people like these children. I assure you that whoever doesn't welcome God's kingdom like a child will never enter it."
> (Luke 18:16-17)

WHAT CAN TEACHERS LEARN FROM KIDS?

Jesus said God's kingdom belongs to people who are like children. For those of us who work with children, it is always exciting and full of unpredictable moments. The learning is mutual. As we teach, we also learn from our kids. We need to recognize and appreciate how much we can learn from observing children.

Enthusiasm: One of the great things about kids is their natural excitement and their love of life. We can maintain the wonder of childhood when we continually venture to try new things.

Acceptance: Younger kids are usually very accepting. They do not hesitate to receive what they are given. They ask for what they want and accept what they are given.

Trust: Kids are generally not too skeptical. They are willing to trust, provided they know that they are leaning on someone worthy of their confidence.

Imagination: Kids have so much wonder and joy in the use of imagination and play. Surely God has equipped us with creativity and delights to see it used to God's glory.

Jesus gave us the first tip for teaching kids: we should be like children. The truth to be taught must be learned through truth already known. This requires the teacher to build on an existing foundation of knowledge possessed by the student. Deep Blue includes a process called scaffolding—laying a foundation and continually building on that foundation.

Deep Blue Teacher Tips

PREPARING TO TEACH

- Know the children you teach. Reflect on the general characteristics for the age group you will be teaching. As you teach the children in your group, you will get to know their specific characteristics. This information will guide the way you teach.

- Develop a resource list of referrals within the church and also outside of the church to help with specific needs. Many churches post a list of supplies needed for Sunday school before each quarter. The church members then have an opportunity to serve the children by bringing items on the list.

- Recruit helpers to do some of the work, such as preparing visuals, setting up the classroom, keeping records, and so forth.

- Start planning early. Begin with "Before You Teach," the personal Bible study in your Leader Guide. Take a look at the learning activities and resources. Begin to think of how you can use Bible conversation and wonder questions during learning activities and reinforce the life application.

- The lesson title and its relationship to the series should be examined to give you the major theme to build your lesson around.

- Reviewing the questions asked as well as the headings and subheadings is helpful in understanding the subject and themes.

- Read and study the Scripture passage thoroughly.

Deep Blue: Teaching with Confidence

- Note the lesson aim by answering three questions:
  - What do I want my kids to know?
  - What do I want my kids to feel?
  - How can my kids and their families apply this to their lives?
- Plan and prepare your session. The best session is a prepared session.
- Always overplan. It's better to run out of time than to run short on a lesson.
- Look over the biblical content early in the week to allow God the opportunity to reinforce the Bible truths in your life.
- Review the session plan for resources you might need to gather that aren't in the church supplies.

NOTE: If you are the person who is asked to teach a Sunday school class fifteen minutes before it begins, take heart! The Deep Blue curriculum is organized in a way that will allow you to pick it up and read it as you teach the class.

READY! SET! TEACH!

- Arrive early. A good rule of thumb is to be in place fifteen minutes before the scheduled time to begin. Arriving early allows time to prepare the room and make sure you have the supplies you need.

Deep Blue Teacher Tips

- Teaching begins when the first child enters the room. Be prepared and be ready for the first child. The Deep Blue curriculum provides activities that can be used as the kids are arriving. Prepare activities that can begin with one child and add others as they arrive.

- Build relationships. The best way to make sure that kids and their families know that you care is by building relationships with them individually. Determine a strategy for getting to know the kids and their families. Understand some general trends that influence your kids and the personal likes and dislikes of individual kids. Learning about their families, schools, sports, and hobbies will help build relationships. Don't forget relationships with parents. Take the time to speak to parents and caregivers, and find opportunities to help equip them to be the spiritual leaders in their kids' lives.

- Be energetic and excited about what you are teaching. This helps get students interested and involved.

- Try new things. Be creative about your teaching.

- If something isn't working during the session, try to change it on the spot. Some ideas include moving around in the classroom, starting a new activity or game, or involving kids in acting out the story.

- Ask questions during the session to allow the kids to become a part of the lesson. Ask wonder questions to help the kids develop their beliefs. These are open-ended questions that require more than a memorized response. Questions that require some personal reflection challenge learners to think and make decisions.

- Ask one question at a time. Avoid confusing learners by asking several questions without allowing time to answer them.

- Address everyone with your question. Questions should be open for anyone to answer.

- Wait for answers. Learners often need a few moments to formulate thoughts or ideas before answering. Allow time for learners to think and respond.

- Provide feedback to responses. Acknowledge answers in some way that lets learners know they are heard.

- Follow some questions with questions. Ask questions that help learners clarify the initial question or help them think more clearly about their answers.

- Challenge learners to find the answers to their own questions. If learners ask questions that suggest they are thinking about something, turn the question back to them with comments such as, "What do you think?" or "Why do you think this?"

- Affirm every child who asks or answers questions.

- Accept all answers. No answer is unimportant. Accept and affirm the comment and continue asking for other answers.

- Admit it when you don't have the answer. One of the most important statements a teacher can make is, "I don't really know the answer," because that's OK.

CLASSROOM MANAGEMENT

- Gain the kids' attention.

- Ask the kids to look at you. Wait until everyone is looking. It's better for teachers to say, "Point your eyes toward me" and wait for compliance, instead of saying, "Stop talking, turn around, and look at me."

- Start with small consequences. When a rule is broken, assign the smallest consequence possible and see if that gets the job done.

- Using appropriate curriculum is a classroom management strategy.

- Assigning age-appropriate work eliminates the risk of kids not being able to do the activities.

- Rehearse transitions. Most disruptions occur between activities.

- Anticipate problems and be creative in preventing or handling them.

- Turn a problematic situation into a positive learning event.

- Find things to appreciate. Start class by looking for things to delight in.

- Create an inclusive environment.

Do

- Set up an ice-breaker with pairs of students who introduce each other.
- Be clear up front about expectations and intentions.
- Use inclusive language.
- Ask for clarification if you're unclear about a kid's question.
- Treat all of your kids with respect and consideration.
- Develop an awareness of barriers to learning (cultural, social, experiential).
- Provide sufficient time and space for kids to gather their thoughts and contribute to discussions.

Don't

- Use certain conventions or language that will exclude some groups from understanding or make them feel uncomfortable.
- Have stereotypical expectations of kids.
- Use (or allow others to use) disrespectful language or tone, or disrespectful nonverbal communication.
- Convey a sense of self-importance or superiority.
- Allow the more verbal participants to take over the conversation.
- Discourage alternate views or counterarguments.

Deep Blue Teacher Tips

COMMUNICATION

- Keep discussions constructive and positive.

- Give all kids a voice. Highlight the value of a diversity of perspectives as an essential part of the process of learning and growing. When one kid dominates the conversation, redirect the discussion to another child or another topic. Kids who are hesitant to talk may feel more at ease in small-group discussions. As the teacher, lay down ground rules that prevent children from interrupting one another or speaking simultaneously. Ask kids who offer unclear statements or questions to give examples of their points. Restate the points for verification. Be patient.

- Use a normal, natural voice. Are you teaching in your normal voice? Raising your voice to get kids' attention is not the best approach, and the stress it causes just isn't worth it. The kids will mirror your voice level. If we want kids to talk at a normal, pleasant volume, we must do the same.

- Change your tone of voice. If you are asking kids to do something, use a matter-of-fact tone. If you are asking a question, use an inviting, conversational tone.

- Speak when students are quiet and ready. Patience pays off, and you'll get to keep your voice.

- Use hand signals and other nonverbal communication. Holding one hand in the air and making eye contact with students is a great way to quiet the class and direct their attention to you. It takes a while for kids to get used to this as a routine, but it works wonderfully. With younger students, try clapping your hands three times and teaching the children to quickly clap back. This is a fun and active way to get their attention and have all eyes on you.

- Address behavior issues quickly and wisely. Be sure to address issues as quickly as possible. Bad feelings can grow rapidly. To handle conflicts wisely, you and the kid involved should step away from the other kids. Avoid interrupting the lesson when possible. Ask questions such as, "How can I help you?"

- Don't accuse the child of anything. Show that you care about the kid's feelings.

- When students have conflicts with each other, arrange for the students to meet with you. Use neutral language as you act as a mediator. Help them resolve the problem peacefully.

- Any correction that you do in class has to be appropriate and it has to make sense to the kids.

- Sometimes the behavior of a single child can become so disruptive that you can't teach your session. Don't let your anger grow out of control; get help! If certain children are repeatedly disruptive, add more adults to your group, or ask parents and caregivers for helpful ways to care for and engage the child.

Deep Blue Teacher Tips

> **NOTE:** Refer to your church's policy on discipline in the classroom. If you have questions about what you can and cannot do in class, you should ask your immediate supervisor.

THE IMPORTANCE OF PLAY

> Play is the business of small children. Through play they find out about their world and how to relate to other persons. In play they express their feelings and ideas. In play they try on what it is like to be another person.[4]

Do childhood departments of both public and Christian education have too much emphasis on play? In some cases, such a criticism may be warranted. But there are two common problems which lead to confusion about this teaching method. The first is a failure to recognize the significance of play activities in the educational process. The second is a failure on the part of some teachers to make play and games genuinely instructive. Almost all toys and play activities should be educational to some extent. They should be promoting the physical, mental, emotional, social, and spiritual development of the child.

An example of instructive play could be using blocks to build a church after the children have heard a story about God's house. Sharing the blocks is as important an experience for the children as thinking about the church they are building.

---

[4] Eleanor Shelton Morrison and Virgil E. Foster, *Creative Teaching in the Church* (Englewood Cliffs, NJ: Prentice-Hall Inc., 1963), 204.

The intuitive teacher will allow sufficient freedom and flexibility in the play process for children to find their own way in certain things. For example, in the modeling of clay, if the children are told to make a particular object, they might attempt to make it as much like the teacher's model as possible or ask the teacher to help them so they will not have an inferior production. If, on the other hand, they are given a lump of clay and asked to make something that would help remind them of the Bible story, a variety of symbols and ideas might result from the creative powers of the children's minds.

> If the children are only talked to, or participate only in activities directed by the teacher, it is difficult for the teacher to know at what points each child is or is not growing in his ability to understand, trust, and love others. It is in the spontaneous interactions of children that a listening, sensitive teacher can find out what progress is being made by a child in living religiously with others.[5]

The weakness in learning through playing comes when it ceases to be instructive, particularly in Christian education, where what we have to communicate is so crucial. We want to be sure that every activity of the classroom, formal or informal, leads toward the accomplishment of worthy objectives.

Possible Questions to Assess Activities

- Was the activity genuinely purposeful or was it just a filler?
- Were new skills developed?
- Was group discussion used?
- Did the activity seem to increase social cooperative behavior?

---

5 Ibid, 198.

Deep Blue Teacher Tips

- Were the children too dependent on the teacher during the playtime?

- If you have used this activity before, did the children show new findings this time?

What are the benefits of learning by playing?

Play is one of the primary ways kids learn.
Play truly is a child's learning lab.

Play can be used to illustrate biblical truth.
Using guided play is one of the most effective ways you can teach kids God's Word.

The play approach helps them to explore their faith through story, to gain religious language, and to enhance their spiritual experience though wonder.

When the foundation of children's character is being formed and developed by play, we partner with caregivers in helping children grow.

Play can be used to practice living out truths.
Through play, you can give kids opportunities to live out what has been taught.

Children make sense of the world in which they live by acting out situations before they happen and by copying what they see around them. Pretend play contributes to a child's emotional development as they learn to see life from a different viewpoint.

Play gives kids the opportunity to connect with one another.
Children thrive when they can experience new materials, roles, ideas, and activities. The children have the opportunity to explore, create, roleplay, and interact with other children.

Play gives kids the opportunity to connect with leaders.
It's important for kids to have some time with leaders to interact and build relationships. While it is very important that children play with their peers and are given opportunities for unstructured play, children who also play with loved adults can benefit greatly.

Play lets kids use their creativity and imagination.
When you allow kids to play, you have a front-row seat to some of the most imaginative theater ever produced.

Play allows kids to engage at their age level.
Whether it's parallel playing or cooperative play, children learn from their peers through play.

Play contributes to a child's well-being.
It gives kids confidence and helps them learn how to make friends.

Play allows kids to learn while they move!
Children are naturally wiggly, and it's important they have space to move around, explore, and express themselves.

Deep Blue Teacher Tips

Play makes church a fun experience for kids.

Teaching becomes a joy when children enter willingly and joyfully into the educational activities we have planned for them. If those educational activities take the form of play, that positive reaction will be gained much more quickly.

Learning Through Playing Activities Used in the Deep Blue Curriculum

- Building with blocks or other items
- Reading books
- Forming items from clay or other malleable resources
- Spiritual practices using methods like bubble-blowing
- Playing with dolls or story figures
- Painting
- Coloring
- Learning centers for free play
- Music instruction using motions, group singing, rhythm bands, and accessories like streamers
- Group collaborative activities
- Art projects
- Acting out stories and rhythms with finger play
- Games structured to reinforce an idea from the story or allow the children to place themselves in the story and wonder what they would do

⑦ Deep Blue Families
at Home and at Church

Emily La Branche Delikat

Spiritual formation and Christian education begins at home. Your Sunday school and children's ministry programs are an extension of and a support for each child's family. Knowing the children in your ministry means knowing their families. Knowing the children in your ministry means knowing and understanding how each child relates to the church family and how the church family relates to him or her. This chapter will help you define a Deep Blue family, and provide resources to help you partner with Deep Blue families at home and at church.

DEEP BLUE FAMILIES AT HOME

Who Are Deep Blue Families?
For those who love and care for them in Sunday school, the center of a Deep Blue family is the child.

Every Deep Blue family home is different. Some children live with birth parents, some live with grandparents, some live with adoptive or foster parents, and some live with stepparents. Some children have parents who are married, some have parents who are divorced, and some have parents who never married. Some children have parents who get along with each other, some have parents who do not, some know both biological parents, and some do not. Family is diverse.

Deep Blue: Teaching with Confidence

Deep Blue families are fun, creative, faithful, and full of love. Deep Blue families are messy, busy, chaotic, tired, busy, overwhelmed, sometimes grumpy, and very busy. But more than anything else, Deep Blue families are beloved children of God.

Because each family in your ministry is unique, each child will come to Sunday school with a different perspective. One of the ways you can honor each child and his or her family is to get to know them. Ask your children and their parents to share more about themselves with their Sunday school leaders. Encourage leaders to ask questions that go beyond the typical demographic questions. Ask open-ended questions such as, "What are you curious about?" or "What does your family like to do when you are not at church?" or "How can we support you?" A reproducible Deep Blue family profile is available on pages 88–89. Encourage families to fill out the profiles together, or you might want to have the Sunday school teacher fill out the profile as he or she interviews the family.

Use the completed profiles to help tailor your Deep Blue ministry. Is Martha curious about nature? Send her a note during the week before learning the parable of the sower that says you can't wait to share the story with her. Is Marcus into playing soccer with his brothers? Invite him to bring his favorite soccer ball and show off his moves when you learn the parable of the ten talents. Does Sam love to read? Invite her to read the Bible story this week. What are some other ways you can use the family profiles?

Deep Blue Families at Home and at the Church

PARTNERING WITH PARENTS AND CAREGIVERS

It is our goal for all Deep Blue kids to: Be with God, Love God and neighbor, Understand themselves as children of God, and Explore faith and the Bible. Because spiritual formation and Christian education begin at home, it is vitally important that Sunday school ministries partner with parents and caregivers in order to meet these goals.

Have I mentioned yet that Deep Blue families are busy? They are often overwhelmingly busy. Resources for and methods of partnering with parents and caregivers need to be simple. Deep Blue families are also loving and hardworking, and desire to do the very best for their children. When giving families resources to use at home, remind them that you are giving them a variety of options to choose from. As you are able, help families discern which resources work for them. Not every resource is helpful for every family. Let's explore some ideas and resources for beginning and strengthening this partnership.

Be with God

- Bible Story Sheets—Send the Bible Story Sheet for the session home with each child. Encourage families to read the stories together and try some of the family activities. These activities help families Be with God together.

- Deep Blue Bibles—The *Deep Blue Toddler Bible Storybook,* the *Deep Blue Bible Storybook,* and the *CEB Deep Blue Kids Bible* are excellent resources to share with families. Encourage parents and caregivers to read with their children.

○ Encourage families to practice silence together. Most families will only be able to observe silence for a few moments at first. Each time, they may decide to stay silent for a little longer. Encourage families to listen for God in the silence, then spend time together allowing each family member an opportunity to share what they heard.

Love God and Neighbor

○ Pray together. Encourage families to try using prayer prompts included in the Bible Story Sheets or the Deep Blue Bibles, praying the Lord's Prayer, or saying a mealtime or bedtime prayer. Prayer is a spiritual discipline that helps us to grow in relationship with God through conversation. There is no right or wrong way to pray.

○ Provide opportunities and resources for families to experience community that is diverse. Recognize the contributions diversity brings to community through a variety of gifts, cultures, physical abilities, and more.

Understand Themselves As Children of God

○ Encourage the inclusion of children and their families in the full life of the local church.

○ Take time each week to encourage and affirm each child and his or her family.

○ Equip children and their families with language that encourages them to speak of each member of the family as a child of God.

Deep Blue Families at Home and at the Church

Explore Faith and the Bible

- *Deep Blue Navigate: A Bible Study Companion for Adults Who Care for Children*—Many parents are discovering the Bible for the first time through the stories their children are taught. *Deep Blue Navigate* is a small-group study for the parents of your Deep Blue kids, exploring the same stories each week. *Navigate* will help encourage and equip parents and caregivers for deeper discussion at home.

- All Hands on Deck—This free downloadable resource can be emailed to parents and caregivers or printed and sent home with the children. All Hands on Deck includes a summary of the Bible story, some Bible background, and an activity or wonder question.

- Deep Blue Apps—The Deep Blue Adventures App includes a parent dashboard that is updated weekly to include the Adventure video. It also includes fun Scripture memory games that children can play at home. The Deep Blue Bible Storybook App is a companion to the *Deep Blue Bible Storybook*. Use the app to scan a Bible story, and watch the corresponding video. Both apps are available in iOS and Android app stores.

- *Deep Blue Kids Bible Dictionary*—This colorful and easy-to-read Bible dictionary is a helpful resource for families as they learn new Bible stories together.

COMMUNICATE WITH PARENTS AND CAREGIVERS

Communication is a key part of your ministry with Deep Blue families. Communication can also be one of the more difficult pieces of ministry. Having a communication plan and a routine will assist you and your team in communicating in a way that is most effective for building relationships. With a wide variety of methods of communication available, each church will need to find a method that works well for their Deep Blue families. The Sample Communication Plan below is a helpful place to start.

Each week include both group and individual family messages. Remind families what the children learned in Sunday school, encourage family faith activities, and give families a preview of what will be happening next week.

SAMPLE COMMUNICATION PLAN

	Social Media and Group Messages	Messages for Individual Children and Families
S	Post an image or story: Today in Sunday school, we learned about . . .	Send "We missed you!" postcards or emails.
M	Ask a wonder question.	
T	Share any important church family announcements.	Send emails or notes of encouragement. When possible, include memories or observations from Sunday.
W	Encourage families to use the Deep Blue Adventures App together.	
T	Post an image or story with the Bible verse from the unit, or a link to the unit song in iTunes.	Send birthday cards to the children who have birthdays in the coming week.
F	Share information about family-friendly events at your church or in your community.	
S	Post an image or story: Tomorrow in Sunday school, we will learn about . . .	

DEEP BLUE FAMILIES AT CHURCH

Who Are Deep Blue Families?
For those who love and care for them in Sunday school, the center of a Deep Blue family is the child. Each child is part of his or her family at home, but every child is also a part of the church family.

Every Deep Blue church family has some things in common. Every church family is a group of people who have come together around their faith. Every Deep Blue church family is intergenerational. Parents and children make up a part of the church family. Who else is in your church family? Are there grandparents, empty-nesters, older adults without children, college students, young professionals, younger to middle-age adults without children? Every Deep Blue church family is made up of people and groups who each have their own needs, desires, and spiritual practices.

PARTNERING WITH THE DEEP BLUE CHURCH FAMILY
It is our goal for all Deep Blue kids to: Be with God, Love God and neighbor, Understand themselves as children of God, and Explore faith and the Bible. This is also an important set of goals for the entire church family. Lead pastors, committees, and other leadership groups have a lot of work to do in helping church families to meet those goals. Sunday school leaders and others in children's ministries get the opportunity to be a voice and advocate for children and families within the larger church community.

Let's explore some ideas and resources for beginning and strengthening a partnership between Deep Blue home families and the church family. These ideas and resources will help the church support, include, value, and encourage children and their families. While every Deep Blue church family has some central things in common, every faith community is also different. Some of these suggestions will be helpful for your congregation, and some will not. You may want to meet together with a group of parents and other church members to discern the best approach for your church family. Consider creating a children's council or leadership team to collaborate on best practices and ideas for your children's ministry.

Be with God

- Worship together. Welcome children into the full life of the church through worship. Every church has their own way of including children in worship. Some churches include children in the entirety of worship services with their families. Some churches include children in the beginning, and sometimes ending, of worship, and take children to a children's church experience during the sermon. Some churches have a children's worship service that is separate from the worship of the rest of the congregation. Some churches have worship and Sunday school simultaneously. No matter the method your church uses, encourage your church family to be intentionally inclusive of children. How can your children serve and lead in worship? In what ways does your church invite children to be with God? In what ways does your church invite children to be with God as a part of the faith community?

_ _ _ _ _ Deep Blue Families at Home and at the Church _ _ _ _ _

- *Deep Blue Kids Church*—This resource will give you some guidance in making your worship time with children a valuable and spiritually forming time, no matter how your community prayerfully chooses to include children in the sanctuary. Each of the thirteen sessions is intended to mirror a typical liturgical sequence. The children will gather, hear a "proclamation," and respond to the story they have heard. Each session also includes a worship practice that will help children understand and learn how to participate in part of a worship service.
- *Piggyback Psalms*—This resource includes over 100 psalms written in child-friendly language and set to familiar tunes. *Piggyback Psalms* can introduce children, their families, and the entire congregation to singing psalms. Use the songs for children's worship, in Sunday school, in intergenerational worship, and at home.

Love God and Neighbor

- Include children in service. When your church engages in churchwide mission projects, be sure to include activities that allow children and their families to participate. This may be filling flood buckets or preparing health kits, writing cards and signs, or helping with community cleanup.
- Encourage children to invite their friends to come to worship and other church activities with them. This gives children the opportunity to be hosts for the church family, and helps them learn to love God and neighbor in a new way.

Understand Themselves As Children of God

- Encourage the inclusion of children and their families in the full life of the local church. Keep them in mind as you plan. Schedule church activities in a way that children and families will be able to participate. Consider avoiding mealtimes, unless eating is included in the activities. Consider children's sleep. Is it possible for you to work around nap and bedtime? Consider the school day and the busy lives of working parents in your planning. That is a lot to consider! Don't worry; not every event can be scheduled this way. The point is to be intentional and to keep children and their families in mind. Parents will notice your effort.

- Find times each week to remind all members of your church family, not just the youngest, that they are children of God. Equip the entire church family with language that encourages them to speak of one another as children of God.

Explore Faith and the Bible

- Consider using the CEB Bible translation in worship so that as the Scriptures are read, the children may easily read along using their *CEB Deep Blue Kids Bibles*. It is OK if your church has pew Bibles that are in a different translation. Adults who choose to follow along will have an easier time doing so with a different translation than children will. Children will benefit greatly from hearing Scripture in the translation they are most familiar with from Sunday school, and even more from being able to read along themselves.

Deep Blue Families at Home and at the Church

- Connecting with Deep Blue—This free resource connects weekly readings from the Revised Common Lectionary with stories that are included in the *Deep Blue Bible Storybook, Deep Blue Adventure DVD* videos, and other Deep Blue resources. In Connecting with Deep Blue, you will also find a summary of the Sunday school session for the coming week and planning helps for the future. This resource is great for sharing with other leaders in your church family, so they can participate in connecting Sunday school to the full life of the church (www.deepbluekids.com/connecting).

COMMUNICATE WITH THE DEEP BLUE CHURCH FAMILY

Communication is a key part of your ministry. Use email, social media, newsletters, and moments in worship to tell the congregation about what the children are learning in Sunday school. Just as you want to be sure to invite the children into the full life of the church, be sure to invite the whole church into the full life of your children's ministry.

Deep Blue: Teaching with Confidence

My Deep Blue Family
Information Form

It is our goal to help children learn to understand themselves and others as children of God. One of the ways that we honor children and their families as children of God is by learning about who they are. Please help your child fill out this information form, and share what you would all like your Sunday school family to know. If your family would like to share something that is best discussed confidentially, please see your teacher.

My Name: _____ My Birthday: _____

I like: _____

_____

I don't like: _____

_____

I am curious about: _____

_____

_____

I live with: _____

_____

These are some people who are special to our family: _____

_____

_____

Permission to reproduce for local church use only. © 2018 Cokesbury.

Deep Blue Families at Home and at the Church

When we are with our church family, we participate in: _____
_____
_____

When my family is not at church, we like to: _____
_____
_____
_____

When we talk about God and faith at home, it looks and sounds like: _____
_____
_____

My family would like support talking about or learning about:
_____
_____
_____

This is the best way to get in touch with my family:

Address: _____

Phone: _____

Email address: _____

Permission to reproduce for local church use only. © 2018 Cokesbury.

Appendix
Using This Resource to
Train Deep Blue Volunteers

This resource was created for you. This includes all who minister to and serve children in your churches and congregations. We encourage you to find methods to use this resource in the ways that best apply to your ministry setting. You could use it as a book study or as a guide for a teacher-training workshop.

TEACHING WITH CONFIDENCE wants to equip and empower teachers and volunteers to have the confidence they need to minister to and serve children. This resource aims to train and educate your volunteers to be partners in ministry by engaging them deeply in the Deep Blue philosophy.

What follows is a training outline for your ministry settings. Training volunteers is essential. Because Deep Blue is a way of doing ministry, training is important and valuable to all those involved. We recommend that all adults in your classroom be trained in these Deep Blue practices as well as in the practices and policies of your church and congregation. Training equips teachers and volunteers with the skills and tools they need to minister to and care for children. Ultimately, a thriving ministry led by adults who understand this philosophy will make for a more effective ministry in serving children and all those who care for them.

VOLUNTEER AND TEACHER TRAINING

Invite your volunteers to gather together for a time of reflection and education. This will be a holistic time for teachers and volunteers to become acclimated to the ways in which children creatively and spiritually interact with Deep Blue resources and curriculum.

Suggested Training Materials

- Samples of the Deep Blue curriculum, including all the age levels and other resources you are using in your ministry
- A copy of this book, DEEP BLUE: TEACHING WITH CONFIDENCE
- Deep Blue Bibles—The *Deep Blue Toddler Bible Storybook,* the *Deep Blue Bible Storybook,* and the *CEB Deep Blue Kids Bible*
- Have the Deep Blue mission statement and B.L.U.E. acronym printed on tables or hung up in the room.

TRAINING 1

Opening

Greet each person as they come into the space, just like you would a child. Offer a gathering activity, such as a coloring sheet, mandala, or puzzle. This mimics a way to help children transition into the classroom. You could also have a reflection question for participants to reflect on and journal about.

Suggested Reflection Questions

- What do you hope to take away from this training?

Using This Resource to Train Deep Blue Volunteers

- How did DEEP BLUE: TEACHING WITH CONFIDENCE expand your understanding of your church's ministry with children?
- Where do you think you can grow in your own ministry with children?

Gather

Once all those attending have arrived, invite everyone to participate in a gathering activity. This can be an icebreaker, a get-to-know-you game, or an activity taken from a Deep Blue lesson. The goal is to help people engage with one another and with the curriculum.

Suggested Gathering Activities

- Share a story from when you were a child in church or Sunday school. How did this experience shape your understanding of God and your faith?
- Invite each participant to make a collage of her or his individual faith journey, and share the collage with a neighbor or with the group. How has your faith journey led you to your ministry with children?
- Bring a large ball of yarn. Invite the group to sit in a circle. Pick a person to start the activity, and invite this person to share one thing he or she hopes to learn from this training. Direct that person to hold on to the loose end of the yarn ball, then pass the yarn to another person in the circle. Continue until everyone has hold of a piece of the yarn and has had a chance to share. When the activity is completed, you should have formed a web of yarn. Close with a discussion about how we are all connected through faith and our ministry to children.

Deep Blue: Teaching with Confidence

Explore

Gather everyone in a circle. Light a candle to symbolize that this is a special and holy time together. Invite participants to wonder together. Use wonder questions that you would use with children.

I wonder:

- How do you feel today?
- What made you laugh today?
- What was a difficult part of your day?
- How have you served others today?
- Where do you see God working today?

(Make up your own questions that are appropriate for your group).

Then, read a Bible story together. It is suggested you read the story from the CEB Bibles used in your Deep Blue classrooms.

Suggested Biblical Texts

- Deuteronomy 6:5-8

Love the Lord your God with all your heart, all your being, and all your strength. These words that I am commanding you today must always be on your minds. Recite them to your children. Talk about them when you are sitting around your house and when you are out and about, when you are lying down and when you are getting up. Tie them on your hand as a sign. They should be on your forehead as a symbol.

Using This Resource to Train Deep Blue Volunteers

- Matthew 19:13-15

Some people brought children to Jesus so that he would place his hands on them and pray. But the disciples scolded them. "Allow the children to come to me," Jesus said. "Don't forbid them, because the kingdom of heaven belongs to people like these children." Then he blessed the children and went away from there.

Respond

After the reading, allow some silent reflection, meditation, and prayer. Ask the group to reflect on the ways in which this text influences their ministry with children. You might make available journaling pages, play dough, art supplies, and other quiet ways for persons to respond.

After ten minutes or more, bring the group back together. Invite willing volunteers to talk about their personal responses.

Have a discussion around the importance of silence, self-reflection, and prayer. Talk about ways these things are important for children and their faith development. How might you incorporate these practices into your ministry with children?

Bless

Close by offering a blessing for each person participating in the training. Just like you would bless each child as she or he leaves the room, offer the same blessing to the adults gathered in the circle. Use unscented lip balm to draw a heart or cross on the top of each participant's hand. Say a blessing such as, "You are a blessing to others, and especially to children."

> **NOTE:** It is also suggested that you find a time in your training to go over your church's safety polices and procedures.

Follow-up
Don't forget to follow up with your volunteers after the training. Check in with them regularly, see what questions or support they might need, and journey alongside them as they do ministry with you and with children.

Use the evaluation found at the end of the book as a way to get feedback from the training and to better assess your ministry with children.

TRAINING 2
Another model for training is to do a book study. Invite volunteers to read this book together. You could offer a weekly small-group discussion or a weekend retreat.

Sometimes the thought of doing a formal book study with others can seem like an extra task, but remember—this is an important training tool. A book study can nurture learning and collaboration, as well as education, for those working in your children's ministry.

A book study can be a powerful tool for developing skilled volunteers. This book creates conversation around the spiritual and theological implications of ministry with children. A guided conversation can help lead to a better-equipped ministry, and can serve as a supportive environment for those working with and serving children in your congregation.

Use the following reflection questions as a guide for conversation.

Using This Resource to Train Deep Blue Volunteers

QUESTIONS FOR REFLECTION

Chapter 1: Deep Blue History, Philosophy, and Theology

- How does the B.L.U.E. acronym influence your ministry with children?

- Where do you see yourself and your ministry in this acronym?

- In what ways does your children's ministry honor each child as a beloved child of God?

QUESTIONS FOR REFLECTION

Chapter 2: Sacred Conversations

- Why is it important to tell stories to children?

- What do you consider sacred?

- How does the Bible influence our faith and the faith of children?

- How could you incorporate midrashic methods of storytelling into your classrooms and ministry?

- Have you ever had a child ask you a difficult question? How did you respond?

Using This Resource to Train Deep Blue Volunteers

QUESTIONS FOR REFLECTION

Chapter 3: Using Deep Blue Resources

- What is your purpose or mission statement for your children's ministry?

- How many children attend your church's Sunday school? What are their ages?

- What Sunday school resource will work best for your ministry?

- What worship resources do you provide for children?

- Do your resources match your mission statement?

Deep Blue: Teaching with Confidence

QUESTIONS FOR REFLECTION

Chapter 4: How to Set Up a Deep Blue Classroom

- What does your dream ministry space look like? What could you do to make this space possible?

- What small changes can you make to create a more intentional and inviting space for children?

- Who could you ask for support in creating a meaningful space for your ministry?

- What supplies do you wish you always had on hand in your classrooms? How can these be obtained?

Using This Resource to Train Deep Blue Volunteers

QUESTIONS FOR REFLECTION

Chapter 5: The Flow of a Deep Blue Session

- Who leads your classes? How can you help this person or persons better incorporate the Deep Blue curriculum model?

- How do you prepare to teach a lesson?

- What parts of the lesson are most challenging for you? Why?

Deep Blue: Teaching with Confidence

QUESTIONS FOR REFLECTION

Chapter 6: Deep Blue Teacher Tips

- What tips did you find most helpful? most challenging?

- What is the most important thing you have ever learned from a child?

- How do you handle conflict and disruption in your ministry?

- Who do you go to for support in your ministry?

- How do you encourage play with children?

Using This Resource to Train Deep Blue Volunteers

QUESTIONS FOR REFLECTION

Chapter 7: Deep Blue Families at Home and at Church

- Name something you are currently doing successfully in your ministry to support families. What makes it successful?

- Name something you are currently struggling with in your ministry to support families. What makes it difficult?

- How frequently do families in your ministry attend Sunday school? What factors affect their attendance?

- What are ways you can create intergenerational programming in your congregation?

CLOSING PRAYER

Loving God,

You have entrusted your beloved children to us. It is a privilege that we do not take lightly.

Thank you for equipping each of us with gifts for ministry. May we follow in the teaching of Jesus and welcome every child.

Sustain me on the days when I am tired, and give me strength to serve with patience, mercy, and grace.

May your Spirit guide me so I can do your creative and courageous work, and may I see the face of God in every child.

Amen.

Using This Resource to Train Deep Blue Volunteers

VOLUNTEER EVALUATION

- What is your role in the life and ministry of children?

- What are the best practices of your children's ministry program? Where do you see weaknesses?

- What do you hope children will gain from your children's ministry programming? from your personal ministry with children?

- How would you like to grow in your own faith and spiritual life?

- Teaching children for me is…

- I could best be supported in my ministry with children by…

Deep Blue: Teaching with Confidence

THANK YOU

On behalf of the entire Deep Blue team, we thank you! We hope this book has helped you experience and feel our commitment to making meaningful resources for children, and our joy in equipping and empowering each of you to do important work and ministry in your church settings. It is a pleasure to work alongside each of you as we explore what it means to be faithful followers of Jesus Christ and to share that message with children. We felt it was important for us to write this book. Together, we wanted to share with you our hearts and our dedication to the work we love.

If you want to continue to be a part of this important work and collaborate with the Deep Blue team, we hope you will follow us on social media, write us emails, and fill out evaluations. We couldn't do this without each of you and your commitment to children and children's ministries. THANK YOU!

www.deepbluekids.com

Follow us @DeepBlueKids

If you have additional questions or if you would like to comment on resources, please call toll free: **800-672-1789**. Or email **customerhelp@cokesbury.com**.

Using This Resource to Train Deep Blue Volunteers

NOTES

Deep Blue: Teaching with Confidence

NOTES

Using This Resource to Train Deep Blue Volunteers

NOTES

Deep Blue: Teaching with Confidence

NOTES